Considerations on the Causes of
THE GREATNESS OF THE ROMANS AND THEIR DECLINE

Considerations on the Causes of
THE GREATNESS OF THE ROMANS AND THEIR DECLINE

MONTESQUIEU

Translated,
with Introduction and Notes, by

DAVID LOWENTHAL

Hackett Publishing Company, Inc.
Indianapolis/Cambridge

Copyright © 1965 by The Free Press

Reprinted with corrections by Hackett Publishing Company, Inc., 1999

Printed in the United States of America

21 20 19 18 17   4 5 6 7 8 9

For further information, please address
  Hackett Publishing Company, Inc.
  P.O. Box 44937
  Indianapolis, IN 46244-0937

  www.hackettpublishing.com

Library of Congress Cataloging-in-Publication Data

Montesquieu, Charles de Secondat, baron de, 1689–1755.
    [Considérations sur les causes de la grandeur des Romains et de leur
décadence. English]
    Considerations on the causes of the greatness of the Romans and
their decline / Montesquieu ; translated, with introduction and notes,
by David Lowenthal.
    p.   cm.
    Includes bibliographical references and index.
    ISBN 0-87220-496-0 (pbk.)—ISBN 0-87220-497-9 (cloth)
    1. Rome—History.   2. Montesquieu, Charles de Secondat, baron
de, 1689–1755.   Considerations sur les causes de la grandeur des
Romains.   I. Lowenthal, David.   II. Title.
DG210.M778   1999
937—dc21   99-28814
                                                                        CIP

ISBN-13: 978-0-87220-496-6 (pbk.)
ISBN-13: 978-0-87220-497-3 (cloth)

CONTENTS

TRANSLATOR'S PREFACE

This work was first published in 1734, not in France but in Holland, and anonymously. Montesquieu revised it himself for the edition of 1748, which is therefore authoritative.

I am aware of two earlier translations into English, one by an Englishman in Montesquieu's own day, the other by an American scholar, Jehu Baker, in 1882. Both have long been out of print. Both are written with more flourish than befits current tastes. Of the two, Baker's is considerably more accurate, and I have occasionally adopted a phrase from it, but it also contains many errors and departs too frequently from an exact rendition of the text.

The function of translators is to translate, not to improve —as they think—upon an author's intelligibility. I have not presumed any incapacity to express himself on Montesquieu's part, or any superiority in my own historical vantage point that might allow me to say better what he thought he had said well enough. My sole purpose has been to reproduce the meaning and fluency of his text as closely as possible. From this rule I have regularly admitted only one deviation: sentences too lengthy or complex to parallel in English have been divided up. All paragraphing, however, is faithful to the original.

The most erudite French editions are those of Camille Jullian (1906) and Henri Barckhausen (1900), but these too have long been unavailable to the public. Two recent editions are those of Gonzague Truc (published by Garnier) and Roger Caillois (in the Pléiade series). The notes by Jullian and Truc are especially helpful, and in all four French editions the interested reader can find Montesquieu's textual revisions. A facsimile of the first edition of Montesquieu's collected works (1758) appeared recently under the editorship of André Masson (published by Nagel).

My own notes are meant merely to be informative, not interpretive, and, for the most part, only on points the reader might have difficulty elucidating for himself. Montesquieu's notes are indicated numerically and are found at the end of each chapter, mine are by letter and at the foot of the page. The references set in parenthesis are taken from Jullian and serve to correct, amplify or supplement those of Montesquieu and thus to help the reader use modern editions of the works he cites. Latin titles and quotations have also been translated, and the Index is the one prepared for the 1748 edition either by Montesquieu himself or under his supervision.

I wish to express my deep gratitude to the editor, Mr. Bloom, to Mrs. Monique Miles, and to my wife for their generous assistance in improving the translation. I am also grateful to Wheaton College for a grant facilitating my studies as well as for the leisure afforded by a sabbatical leave of absence. I am delighted that this political masterpiece has found a second home among the Hackett Classics.

David Lowenthal
Princeton, Mass.

INTRODUCTION

i

Montesquieu's *Considerations on the Causes of the Greatness of the Romans and Their Decline* was published almost midway between his *Persian Letters* (1721) and *The Spirit of the Laws* (1748). Today it is the least well known of the three, though not through any fault of its own. It may have been the first (and certainly was one of the first) of all efforts to comprehend the whole span of Roman history, and among such efforts it still has few if any peers—even after a century and a half of the scientific historiography Montesquieu's own writings did so much to engender, and which has now grown disdainful of its philosophic forbears. It was probably one of the works Gibbon had in mind in his *Memoirs* when he wrote: ". . . but my delight was in the frequent perusal of Montesquieu, whose energy of style, and boldness of hypothesis, were powerful to awaken and stimulate the genius of the age." But the context in which it must be understood, and from which it derives its chief value, is not that of history but of political philosophy. In the annals of this subject, it is one of the few instances when a philosopher has undertaken an extended analysis of any particular society, let alone of its entire history. The only comparable thing on Rome is Machiavelli's *Discourses*, to which it bears a deep inner kinship. But it is simpler than the *Discourses*, both in structure and meaning. For the most part it uses an historical framework, beginning with Rome's origins and ending with its collapse, and its teaching is in some ways less devious.

Not that the *Considerations* automatically empties itself into the reader's mind; on the contrary, it is written with a care—indeed, a caution—which its apparent simplicity and directness belie, and only the penetrating and reflective reader will catch sight of its depths. The work is less than candid. In fact, it does not even vouchsafe its own purpose, and in this respect differs markedly from Montesquieu's other two main works. It has no preface, and there is no statement of intent elsewhere in the text. Its purpose must therefore be inferred. Its unusually informative title indicates that Montesquieu is not primarily interested in presenting a general history of Rome, or even a history of its greatness and decline, but an account of the *causes* of that greatness and decline. And it is the *Romans*—an entity transcending particular political forms—not their republic or empire as such that is under study.

In a manner becoming a political observer of political life, Montesquieu makes no attempt in the text to set forth obtrusive "scientific" definitions of greatness and decline. He uses the term "greatness" with fair frequency, "decline" more sparingly. "Greatness" conveys the idea of large size and also of power (let us call these its physical and political meanings, respectively). As Rome grows larger and more powerful, it becomes greater. But power is the crux of a nation's greatness, and a multitude of examples suggest that, for Montesquieu, power is nothing but the ability to coerce other nations. Correspondingly, the chief meaning of "decline" is increased weakness.

The third, or moral, aspect of "greatness" is related to, but not identical with, the political. Roman power derived from Roman virtue, *i.e.*, from great moral qualities. The average Roman was simple, steadfast, honest, courageous, law-abiding, and patriotic; and his leaders were men of unusual dedication and acumen. Now these virtues had their origin in the particular circumstances of a small society constantly at war for its life, and Montesquieu never regards them in terms of a natural perfection toward which mankind is drawn. Nevertheless, they elicit his unabashed admiration and are treated as elements not merely of Roman but of *human* greatness. Somehow these virtues have a status rising beyond the particularity of their origin and befitting man as such, but we are never told the reasons why.

Although Montesquieu seems to consider the moral virtues intrinsically valuable and not simply socially useful, he does associate them especially with the political life of small republics, and with the ancient city in particular. His portrait of the city is vivid and profound. Few moderns have rivaled it, and those who have, such as Rousseau and Fustel de Coulanges, were inspired by it. He shows us the city's link to the gods, its sense of common destiny and long-established custom, its sharing of a common life; he lets us see how the free Roman citizen, through participation in fighting and ruling, developed a keen sense of personal pride and patriotic ambition; he reveals the discord between the higher and lower elements of Roman society, and its consequences. Amid such circumstances, the ancient republic both nurtured, and was nurtured by, moral virtues. The result was a powerful state; indeed, Montesquieu implies that nothing can match a republic for sustained conquest, *i.e.,* for the steady augmentation of political power and greatness, as in the case of Rome.

ii

Rome's power first revealed itself under the early kings and rose to its height under the republic, apparently with Pompey (*c.* 65 B.C.), who ". . . completed the splendid work

empire =
roman
empire

of Rome's greatness." But by that time Rome's internal corruption had become manifest and irremediable, and the republic could no longer endure. It was replaced by the empire,
which maintained itself largely by means of habits and institutions inherited from the republic. Because of these and
other factors, it was only after the end of the third century
that the empire ". . . went, by slow degrees, from decline to
fall, until it suddenly collapsed under Arcadius and Honorius."
(*c.* 400 A.D.)

If, as Montesquieu tells us, Pompey's foreign conquests
did not really increase Rome's power, real and apparent greatness must be distinguished. Mere size, and even continuing
conquests, do not suffice as indices of a nation's real power.
Its enemies of the moment may be weak; its magnitude may
burden rather than assist it. In the long run, and at bottom,
a nation's strength depends on the state of its internal health.
It is hard to say when Rome reached the height of its real
power. The civil wars of the first century B.C. assisted rather
than obstructed its conquests, but they gave evidence of a
deepseated decay that ultimately had to reduce Roman power
by destroying the republic. In one place, Montesquieu gen-
erally dates this decay from the time of Rome's expansion
beyond Italy, and in another specifies that ". . . the war
they waged against Antiochus is the true beginning of their
corruption." This would mean that the republic began to
decline internally from about 200 B.C. onward, and that its
corruption was completed in one and a half centuries.

Rome's greatness had many causes: the virtue of its
citizens, the system of consuls, the senate's wisdom, the limited
influence of the people, the concentration on war, the triumphs, the public sharing of booty, the equal partition of
land, the censorship, the broad distribution of political power.
The people were imbued with a passionate and indomitable
love of country, and the senate sustained a military and foreign policy that led unceasingly to the defeat and subjection

of Rome's enemies. Thus, once formed, it was the republican order, not particular individuals, that made Rome great, and, in Montesquieu's account, individuals hardly regain prominence till this order breaks down.

Rome's decline was the result of its conquests. The waning of public spiritedness in distant Roman generals and soldiers, the growing inequality of wealth and power, with extremes of luxury and poverty, the exacerbation of faction, the loss of a sense of common identity among Romans as citizenship was extended to other peoples—these made it impossible to preserve the republic. Montesquieu also draws attention to the corroding effect of Epicureanism on Roman morals, implying that the spread of its atheistic materialism and hedonism helped destroy religious and moral beliefs upon which Roman patriotism and virtue depended.

Montesquieu judges the empire by the moral and political standards of the republic, thereby making clear the general human decline that, in his view, occurred with the transition from one to the other. At first the empire was more wanting in liberty, security, and virtue than in external power. While tyranny intensified from Augustus to Caligula, an effort was made to preserve the territory of the empire in peace. And as the emperors became increasingly arbitrary, harsh and fear-ridden, both the senate and the people—stripped of their political function and dignity—became slavish and despicable. Yet, especially in the span from Nerva to the Antonines (96-180 A.D.), the empire had its glorious moments. The highest praise of any man in the entire book is reserved for the emperor Trajan—"the most accomplished prince in the annals of history." Montesquieu also extols Marcus Aurelius, and refers admiringly to the Stoic sect which, in contrast to Epicureanism, had helped produce such rulers. After the Antonines, however, the empire degenerated into a tyranny of armies and then a more subtle and withdrawn tyranny of emperors. It recovered from third century barbarian invasions, but then divided the imperial authority and split into an East and a West (*c.* 300 A.D.). Ultimately, the ancient Roman military virtues and practices were themselves abandoned, and marauding barbarians overran the West (400 A.D.).

iii

By deciding to concentrate on the theme of Rome's greatness or power, Montesquieu already shows that he has decided the crucial philosophical question against Plato and Aristotle and in favor of Machiavelli. If the proper yardstick for measuring political worth is power, it cannot be moral goodness as such. He must therefore eschew the kind of moral criticism the Greek political philosophers leveled at Sparta and Cicero leveled at Rome. Departing from the "utopian" standards of the classics and adopting Machiavelli's "realism," he must be willing to sacrifice moral virtue to political greatness at crucial points. Especially in a nation's external conduct but also in its internal affairs, too much by way of moral virtue is not to be expected or sought. Thus, Rome's dedication not only to war but to aggressive conquest, its nefarious practices in foreign policy, its use of slavery, its internal factiousness must either go without serious criticism or receive express approval.

At one point, while analyzing the causes of Rome's ruin, Montesquieu states that Rome could have remained a republic had it not sought domination beyond the borders of Italy. And he does indeed advise wise republics to hazard neither good fortune nor bad, and to perpetuate their condition without expanding. Soon afterward, however, he takes it for granted that the necessary result of "good laws" in a small republic is to cause it to conquer other states and grow larger, until it reaches the point where it can no longer retain

a republican form of government. Here republican imperialism
is accorded something approaching a necessary and natural
status, and this supposition, coupled with Montesquieu's admiration for Roman greatness and the means by which it was
achieved, differs little in its net effect from Machiavelli's
forthright support of such imperialism.

Machiavelli had let the decision concerning the internal
make-up of a properly constituted republic depend on whether
the republic would be nonexpansionist, like Sparta and Venice,
or expansionist, like Rome. Pondering this alternative, he
recognized that the expansionist republic could not avoid
civil discord between nobles and people, since the people,
growing in size, would be emboldened by their military importance to struggle with the nobles for supremacy. He decided in favor of adopting the Roman course from the outset,
on the ground that necessity would at some point probably
compel the Spartan type either to engage in an expansion for
which it was utterly unfit, or to be weakened by excessive
freedom from war; a steady middle way between these alternatives was impossible. To avoid these risks, therefore, it is
better to begin with an expansionist, and factious, republic.
Montesquieu, by contrast, does not even seem to admit the
Spartan alternative. He acknowledges that both Rome and
Sparta exemplify the most powerful kind of republic, the
kind based on passion, or patriotism; but he flatly denies
that a free republic can be composed of soldiers and yet be
lacking in civil discord (as Sparta was). This makes the
Roman solution seem even more natural than in Machiavelli.

The best regimes devised by classical political philosophy
were meant to embody the highest possibilities of human
existence. Although they would be strong, their chief objective
was neither conquest nor war but rather a life of nobility,
pursued in a civic setting where the best men had the pre-
dominant voice and where harmony and stability prevailed.
The preservation of these regimes from the risks of defeat

in war and decay in peace could not be absolutely guaranteed, though it could be reasonably well provided for. Nor were such political conceptions to be abandoned because of the difficulty of the moral training they required, or the rarity of the circumstances under which they would be practicable. But Machiavelli, followed later by Montesquieu, was impatient with demands and risks that had their source in a conception of human virtue higher than that practiced by any state whatsoever. Once both men had decided they could not criticize a Spartan-type dedication to war, they were led to reject Spartan defensiveness in favor of Roman aggression, and hence to support the unequalled political greatness of imperialistic Rome.

The encouragement thus given to the imitation of Rome does indeed eliminate certain risks and demands. However, it also guarantees that the republic involved will be constantly risking its survival in the wars it seeks, constantly embroiled in civil discord, and inevitably transformed into some kind of tyranny should its imperialism prove successful. And this is wholly apart from the general impetus given to the bellicosity of states by such a teaching, and to impractical attempts to create a Roman-type republic. To make such choices for the sake of being more realistic and avoiding chance evils would assuredly have been decried by the classics. Chance, and a prudent use of the conception of human excellence, were kinder masters than these harsh, self-imposed necessities. And it is less compromising to one's love of moral greatness and republican advantages in general to see a good republic go down by chance than to see it subverted by a tyranny made necessary by one's own initial choice of expansionism.

Such are the costs of distinguishing political from moral greatness, and of making the former the supreme political objective rather than the latter. Machiavelli could do so because of his view that the moral virtue of classical philosophy had no basis in human nature. But Montesquieu seems intent on preserving the dignity of moral virtue even while refusing to follow the classics in making it the direct object of political life. The best evidence of this is his glowing tribute to Trajan, which begins by calling Trajan a great statesman and general, then acclaims his noble, great, and beautiful soul and his virtues, and ends by describing him as "the man most suitable for honoring human nature, and representing the divine." Here Montesquieu implies that the best of all princes is the best of all men, and that moral virtue displayed in ruling constitutes the chief end of man and the chief criterion of human greatness.

This panegyric sounds more classical than Machiavellian, and the feelings of tenderness to which Montesquieu confesses on reading about Marcus Aurelius—like his earlier testimonial to the friendships of Cicero and the last republicans—is certainly not in the style of Machiavelli. Nevertheless, Montesquieu does not make a classical use of the virtue he admires and loves. The life of full virtue is not taken as the model for the life of political societies. Trajan himself is depicted as a conqueror, and even the Stoicism of Marcus Aurelius is praised for its moral and political effects but not for its intrinsic merits as a philosophy, or for the act of philosophizing as such. In short, we are given no glimpse of an excellence grounded in contemplation rather than action from which the latter receives inspiration, guidance, and restraint. Warlike action, not rational thought, is the model for human societies. This bears out the Aristotelian insight linking an interest limited to action and politics to an interest in war. Ultimately, then, it is not possible that Montesquieu, any more than Machiavelli, believed man to be fitted by nature for a life of reason and virtue, or that political life lends itself to their guidance. But if moral virtue is not in accord with man's nature, what is the source of its value? And must not this justification be made clear if virtue is not to suffer a mortal wound from the new teaching?

iv

Whereas the choice of Rome over Sparta was made behind the scenes, so to speak, Montesquieu is more open about showing the nature of Rome's superiority to Carthage. Carthage, we may remember, had been regarded by Aristotle, less than a century before the First Punic War, as perhaps the best of all actual regimes, better even than Sparta. He had not called attention to its mercantile character and imperialism, any more than he had to its being a non-Greek or "barbarian" city. But among its defects he had numbered its stress on wealth and also certain powers of the popular assembly. According to Montesquieu, Carthage's main weakness relative to Rome lay in defects of a similar kind, deriving from its mercantile character and the excessive power wielded by its people. Rome, on the other hand, was not a commercial power, and its imperialism stemmed mainly from ambition rather than avarice. Its moral virtue, its devotion to war, its constancy and unity in war, its wise leadership could therefore be greater than Carthage's, and these, in the long run, prevailed. Nevertheless, the threat to Rome mounted by Carthage was graver than any thereafter, and Montesquieu saves the superlative "finest spectacle presented by antiquity" for the exploits of the Carthaginian, Hannibal. Eventually, however, the imperialistic commercial republic proved inferior in power to the imperialistic noncommercial or agricultural republic, and suffered extinction at its hands.

While following Machiavelli's approval of fraud and force in the international arena and adopting his enthusiasm for the imperialistic noncommercial republic, Montesquieu

avarice
↳ greed for wealth or material gain

refuses to follow him in teaching the use of fraud and force for the purpose of obtaining or maintaining tyrannical rule, or in advocating private wickedness. Instead, he constantly and severely criticizes tyrants for the harm they inflict upon their country, and he never gives positive encouragement to the clever cruelty of princes or individuals. In a few cases he may possibly intimate a willingness to overlook grave misdeeds on the part of great and ruthless men—as, for example, in what he says and does not say about Tarquin, Caesar and even Severus—but his reticence in doing so lends even greater emphasis to his modification or correction of Machiavelli. The principle he seems to adopt is that the responsible political philosopher or statesman must always seek to promote the common good, not some merely private good, and must also do as little as possible to promote the cause of tyranny, which for all normal purposes is the worst of possible regimes.

Although Montesquieu can glorify the monarchical rule of a Trajan or a Marcus Aurelius, the regime he considers the source of Rome's political and moral greatness is the republic. It is, moreover, a regime in transition from an aristocratic to a democratic republic, under the stress of civil discord. Unlike the classics, Montesquieu is not averse to the idea of a factious community in principle; commotion can be part of its proper working. He even finds a cosmological basis for the idea in the action and reaction that keep the heavenly bodies in their course—a derivative from Newtonian physics. But his discussion in this place of the desirability of contending groups in Rome is less explicit than Machiavelli's; he is less willing to admit candidly that the "true peace" at which Rome's harmony of dissonances aimed was the constant subjection of its neighbors and rivals.

In his discussions of Rome's internal politics, Montesquieu does not appear to be an enthusiastic democrat, or even, like Machiavelli, a supporter of the justness of the people's cause

as over against the cause of the patricians or nobles. He does
suggest that the most fortunate republics are those without
an hereditary privileged class, but in so doing he stresses
the simple fact that such a class is detested by the people,
not that it practices injustices deserving popular detestation.
And in outlining Rome's internal conflicts, he remains
strangely aloof, again without taking the side of the people
against the privileged groups. The main exception to this
rule is forceful but not express: he quotes from a speech by
the ill-fated Tiberius Gracchus adjuring the nobles to be
less avaricious for land, and thus implies criticism of the
oligarchical tendencies of the dominant class. In general,
however, he is less explicitly critical of the rich and wellborn
than Aristotle himself. At the same time, although perfectly
aware of the virtues of the Roman people, he always recog-
nizes the superior and leading virtues of the senate, and sees
that the immoderate liberty and power of the people is a
great evil. In short, Montesquieu seems to favor a republic
where the people have enough power to protect themselves
against grave injustices but insufficient power to direct the
state. That task must be left to a body of men who make it
their main occupation, and who, by the scope and continuity
of their experience, are able to sustain well-reflected policies
for generations. Here the views of Montesquieu and the
classics approach each other—if we discount the imperialism
he would have the senate pursue as its highest goal. But
Montesquieu would claim that it is this very dedication to
conquest that serves to engender the other advantages of
which this republic can boast—its internal liberty and security, its moral virtue, and, indeed, the prominence of its
senate.

conclusion

v

In the most theoretical statement of the *Considerations,* Montesquieu asserts that general moral and physical causes, not chance or particular causes, rule the world and account for Rome's greatness and decline. It is impossible for us to inquire here as to how he would have defined the basic terms involved, or to ask whether his thesis allows sufficient room for the actions of great individuals or the effects of chance. Nevertheless, it is clear that no sense of physical, historical or divine teleology pervades the work. Montesquieu approaches Rome as an entirely "natural" phenomenon in the modern sense of the term, with a beginning, middle, and end that are more clearly discernible, and more impressive, than in the case of other nations, and that requires to be explained by some combination of general and particular causes. He seems to write as a Cartesian who, unlike Descartes himself and Pascal after him, refuses to abandon the realm of human affairs to particularity, chance and the unintelligible. As to the role in this scheme of divine or supernatural powers, miracles—or, more broadly, divine acts of particular providence—are never dwelled upon and barely alluded to. Nor is there any place among general "moral" causes for divine influence. The only "moral," as opposed to "physical," causes seem to consist in man's varying ideas and the institutions, habits and ways of doing things directly connected with them; ideas about morality are only one of many kinds of ideas or moral causes. And we are never told how, as a matter of theoretical principle, moral and physical causes are related to each other. The work naturally concentrates on moral or human causes, though without ignoring the effects of such physical things as climate, geography and terrain. And of the diverse kinds of moral causes, Montesquieu is mostly interested in those bearing on the critical problems of Roman life, and hence in those that are political. He is very sensitive to the influence of social, economic, military, technological, intellectual, religious, and other kinds of moral causes, but always because of the light they throw on the nature and behavior of the Roman body politic. The political community, and nothing else, is assumed to be the core of human life.

Not only is the *Considerations* conceived in independence of religion: it has a strong anti-Christian animus as well. This is most manifest in its sympathetically reviving the image of Rome's greatness, but more particular indications of the same intent also abound, both in what Montesquieu says and fails to say. Not long after displaying a remarkable openness to the motives underlying pagan suicide, for example, he declares Trajan "the man most suitable for honoring human nature, and representing the divine," and then is unstinting in his praise of the Stoics, whom he distinctly links with nature and human nature rather than with the Christian God. On the other hand, such crucial Christian (and Roman) events as the birth of Christ, the spread of Christianity, the persecutions it suffered, its toleration by Constantine, and Julian's apostasy are buried in a tomb of silence—never directly recounted and seldom mentioned at all. The reader has settled into what is almost complete ignorance of the very existence of Christianity when Chapter XIX—the one on Attila and the collapse of the West—suddenly opens with a topic not even indicated by the chapter title. The topic is the argument that raged at the time between pagans and Christians over Christianity's responsibility for Rome's collapse. After presenting the pagan position in somewhat greater detail than the Christian, Montesquieu attributes to St. Augustine the view that ". . . the ancient Romans, for some human virtues, had received rewards that were as vain as these virtues." He does not try to settle the argument directly, but this quotation shows the significance of his own work with

beautiful conciseness. The whole issue is then abruptly
dropped as he goes on to display an unusual fascination for
the person and accomplishments of Attila the Hun.

The criticism of Christianity begins to mount in the following chapter on Justinian, and it rises to a crescendo in
the three final chapters on what Montesquieu calls the Eastern
or Greek (not Roman) empire. He contrasts the tolerance
of pagan Rome with the Christian Justinian's extermination
of dissenting Christian and non-Christian sects. He describes
the heresy-hunting of the Greeks, and their loss of obedience
to their princes. He refers to the Christian trend toward
slackening the punishment of crimes not directly involving
religion, including rebellion. In accounting for the rapid conquest of parts of the Christian Eastern empire by Moham-
medanism, he quotes "a celebrated author" to the effect that
sickness, or weakness, is the true state of a Christian, and far
from denying it, applies the maxim to the condition of the
Christian church, claiming that the church is at its real
height when its worldly extension and power are minimal,
i.e., when it is "sickest." He depicts the small-mindedness
of the Greeks, their superstition and bigotry, their endless
religious turmoil, their faintheartedness, and, finally, their
neglect of political action, even to the point of jeopardizing
survival.

Montesquieu concludes his criticism of the Greeks by
speaking of the fundamental need to distinguish ecclesiastical
from secular power. He approvingly adduces the old Roman
solution to the problem, which, while distinguishing the two
kinds of power, amounted to having no independent clergy
and giving supreme religious authority to the highest political
authority. We must conclude, therefore, that Montesquieu
considered Christianity a contributory cause of the Roman
empire's decline (West and East), just as Epicureanism had
contributed to the decline of the republic. But the empire
was in decay without it, and the main reason for dwelling

upon the connection between the Greek empire and Christianity is to illumine the essential effect of Christianity on political life. This is why a work considering the greatness and decline of the *Romans* ends with three chapters explicitly devoted to the *Greeks*. The otherworldly Greeks—meaning Christianity in its most unrestrained form—are the diametrical opposites of the Roman republic.

In acclaiming the political life of ancient Rome, Montesquieu does more than spurn classical political philosophy and Christianity: he apparently rejects modern theory and practice as well. Remarks in which he approves of anything modern are infrequent and usually incidental. He does evince admiration for such things as improvements in marine navigation, the role of communications technology in preventing conspiracies against the state, the destiny of the Swiss republic of Bern, the more limited powers of modern European monarchs as compared to the Roman emperors, and the self-correction inherent in the English government. He credits gentler manners and a "more repressive" religion (*i.e.,* Christianity) with making impossible the imperial Roman practice of putting citizens to death in order to confiscate their property. He admits the Romans made sport of human nature in their treatment of children and slaves, and lacked "this virtue we call humanity," yet at the same time strongly criticizes the inhuman colonial practices of modern European powers. His analysis of self-love has an anti-Christian but also a peculiarly modern ring, as does his assertion that the most legitimate basis for a people's acquiring sovereign power over itself consists in its right to self-preservation. But apart from such traces of reservations in favor of post-Machiavellian political philosophy, humanitarianism, and technological and political possibilities that rise superior to the imperialistic polis—reservations that are only permitted to triumph in *The Spirit of the Laws*—the *Considerations* cannot be characterized as anything but a monument to pagan republican

Rome. Implicitly, however, it is also a monument to the modern genius of Machiavelli, who was the first philosopher to dare supply the true understanding and justification of Roman greatness.

vi

The *Considerations* is an inquiry into the greatness and decline of Rome that is cast in the form of a history, proceeding from Rome's origins to its end, and even beyond its end. But the purpose Montesquieu reveals in his title would not require such a structure. Had he wanted to, he could have presented a summary view of the causes of Rome's greatness and decline, as he actually does in many chapters. Instead, he chooses to follow the history, sketching in its most significant features or drawing attention to them by omission, and making what must have been a rather novel use of extensive footnoting, much in the manner of more recent scholarship. It would seem, then, that in order to explain the general and particular causes of Rome's historical saga, that saga had first to be ascertained in its reality and established as an accepted subject matter. Its various parts, its various aspects had first to be gathered together and freed of the heavy incrustation of prejudice built up over centuries. They had also to be seen in the light of new and shocking principles attacking both the religious and philosophic traditions. The notes are therefore important not only for supplying the demonstrative evidence required in historical studies but for calling men back to the original sources and alerting them to those novelties of interpretation Montesquieu could not express unguardedly.

Since the work is little given to overt practical recommendations for Montesquieu's own day and even less to overt theoretical reflection, its surface appearance is closer in sub-

stance as well as form to history and a limited kind of
political philosophy. On the one hand, the overall impression
it leaves is a stimulus not to political innovation or even
participation but to something more like sad, scholarly with-
drawal from politics. For it is indeed melancholy to watch
the "eternal city" perish. It is melancholy to contemplate
the "spectacle of things human," whereby Rome's republican
virtues are seen leading inexorably to imperial tyranny. It
is melancholy to see Roman greatness reduced to Greek decadence, and to lose cosmological and political optimism with
the realization that all human things grow and die untended
by higher powers of any kind.

Nevertheless, beneath its historical exterior, and on the
very nutriment of disillusion, the *Considerations* quite per-
ceptibly revives the conception of a political life that is both
pagan and republican, rather than Christian and monarchical,
that admires ancient rather than Christian virtue, republican
equality rather than monarchical inequality, republican patriotism rather than monarchical honor, and that approves
imperialism on the Roman model. We may therefore discern
in the work an effort to achieve both theoretical and practical
effects: theoretical, by teaching, however indirectly, the true
standard of political greatness and, therewith, the nature
of political things; practical, by preparing minds and hearts
for action in the style of the ancients should the occasion
ever arise. But exactly what Montesquieu purported by this
double influence remains unclear. He never openly indicates
what the practical possibilities of restoration are, or might
become. To be sure, his single most extensive comment on
modern society is ostensibly devoted to showing how the new
technology of communications and commerce drastically reduces the possibility of conspiratorial revolutions against
princes. Yet his strange euphemism for such conspiracies is
"great enterprises," he omits considering the impact of modern weapons (such as guns and bombs), and he leads the

reader to think of the sanctity of rulers in terms of nothing but
the precedents established in different nations. Thus, in spite
of its colorations as "mere history," the work may have had
the effect of encouraging in its readers an incautious contempt
for their own society and arousing groundless or excessive
hopes. It may, in short, have contributed to the initial growth
of that radical, secular republicanism partly modeled on Rome
that later showed itself so violently in the French Revolution.
By comparison, the republicanism of *The Spirit of the Laws*
is meant to be, and is, much more prudent. It is kinder to
the possibilities of modern monarchy; it delineates the special
conditions required for a successful republic; it strongly
criticizes republican imperialism; and it opens up a modern
alternative (England) superior to the ancient republic as
such. Nevertheless, the *Considerations,* by the very glare of
its relatively rash concentration, does more than any other
of Montesquieu's works to reveal the Machiavellian foundations of his thought, and to ready the public for his later
innovations.

This study of Rome has a particular utility for us in the
West today. The societies of the West are living embodiments
of the modern representative republic first rationally conceived by Locke and then elaborated by Montesquieu himself. This daring quasi-English republic was to be based on
liberty and commerce rather than virtue, and was to empha-
size the private life rather than communal solidarity. Montesquieu's own portrait of Rome serves to remind us of one of
the great alternatives to such a republic, and gives prominence to some of the qualities most lacking, and missed in it.
Among these are moral integrity, and, in general, the more
severe virtues; dedication to the public weal; and the will and
capacity to subdue foreign foes. But the broader significance
of the *Considerations* is that it helps remind us of the great
issues separating classical, Christian and modern thought—
issues which were uppermost in Montesquieu's mind, but of

which we are only dimly aware. By picturing ancient political practice against the background of Machiavellian political principles, it especially forces us to re-examine the original alternative to this combination: classical political philosophy. Above all, it inspires us to imitate the author and those like him who sought the fullest truth about things human, who ruled out no vital question, and whose voices fail to move only those whose vanity has already rendered them immobile.

ABOUT THE NOTES

Montesquieu's notes are numbered and follow each chapter. The numbers in parentheses are those supplied as aids to the reader from the French edition of Camille Jullian. Roman and Arabic numerals stand for book and chapter, respectively. The translator's notes are lettered and fall to the foot of the page.

CHAPTER I

1. BEGINNINGS OF ROME

2. ITS WARS

We should not form the same impression of the city of Rome in its beginnings [a] as we get from the cities we see today, except perhaps for those of the Crimea, which were built to hold booty, cattle and the fruits of the field. The early names of the main places in Rome are all related to this practice.

The city did not even have streets, unless you call the continuation of paths that led to it by that name. The houses were located without any particular order, and were very

---

[a] Montesquieu, oddly enough, cites no dates. Of the twenty-three chapters, seven are clearly general or nonchronological in content (II, III, VI, VIII, IX, X, and XVIII). Present historians would date the stretch of events covered by the others in something like the following manner: I (753-387 B.C.); IV (fourth century to 201 B.C.); V (201-168 B.C.); VII (89-63 B.C.); XI (first half of first century B.C.); XII (44-42 B.C.); XIII (42 B.C. to 14 A.D.); XIV (14-37 A.D.); XV (37-138 A.D.); XVI (138-282 A.D.); XVII (285-378 A.D.); XIX (end of fourth century and second half of fifth century A.D.); XX (527-565 A.D.); XXI (565-610 A.D.); XXII (610-1300 A.D.); XXIII (seventh century to 1400 A.D.). Chapters XXI and XXII are both historical and general.

small, for the men were always at work or in the public square, and hardly ever remained home.

But the greatness ᵇ of Rome soon appeared in its public edifices. The works ¹ which conveyed and today still convey the strongest impression of its power were produced under the kings. Already the Romans were beginning to build the eternal city.

To obtain citizens, wives and lands, Romulus and his successors were almost always at war with their neighbors. Amid great rejoicing they returned to the city with spoils of grain and flocks from the conquered peoples. Thus originated the triumphs, which subsequently were the main cause of the greatness this city attained.

Rome markedly increased its strength by its union with the Sabines—a tough and warlike people, like the Lacedaemonians from whom they were descended. Romulus ² adopted their buckler, which was a large one, in place of the small Argive buckler he had used till then. And it should be noted that the main reason for the Romans becoming masters of the world was that, having fought successively against all peoples, they always gave up their own practices as soon as they found better ones.

In those days in the republics of Italy it was thought that the treaties they made with a king did not bind them toward his successor. This was a kind of law of nations for them.³ Thus, whoever had fallen under the domination of one Roman king claimed to be free under another, and wars constantly engendered wars.

ᵇ I have, throughout, translated *grandeur* and *décadence* by "greatness" and "decline" because "grandeur" and "decadence" have a somewhat more specialized meaning today. On the other hand, I have retained "considerations" in the title, despite its rarity today, because Montesquieu himself seems to distinguish it, in some his titles, from the more common "reflections."

Numa's long and peaceful reign was ideal for keeping Rome in a state of mediocrity, and if it had then had a less limited territory and greater power, its fate would probably have been decided once and for all.

One of the causes of its success was that its kings were all great men. Nowhere else in history can you find an uninterrupted succession of such statesmen and captains.

At the birth of societies, the leaders of republics create the institutions; thereafter, it is the institutions that form the leaders of republics.

Tarquin seized the throne without being elected by either the senate or the people.[4] Power was becoming hereditary: he made it absolute. These two revolutions were soon followed by a third.

In violating Lucretia, his son Sextus did the sort of thing that has almost always caused tyrants to be expelled from the city they ruled. Such an action makes the people keenly aware of their servitude, and they immediately go to extremes.

A people can easily endure the exaction of new tributes: it does not know whether some benefit may come to it from the use to which the money is put. But when it receives an affront, it is aware of nothing but its misfortune, and begins thinking of all the possible evils to which it may be subjected.

It is true, however, that the death of Lucretia was only the occasion of the revolution which occurred. For a proud, enterprising and bold people, confined within walls, must necessarily either shake off its yoke or become gentler in its ways.[c]

---

[c] The French word *moeurs* signifies the "morals," "moral customs," "manners" or "ways" of societies and individuals; it refers to both expected and actual behavior, as well as to the inner character of which they are expressions. In each case I have used one of these four terms to express its meaning, depending on context.

One of two things had to happen: either Rome would change its government, or it would remain a small and poor monarchy.

Modern history furnishes us with an example of what happened at that time in Rome, and this is well worth noting. For the occasions which produce great changes are different, but, since men have had the same passions at all times, the causes are always the same.

Just as Henry VII, king of England, increased the power of the commons in order to degrade the lords, so Servius Tullius, before him, had extended the privileges of the people [5] in order to reduce the senate. But the people, at once becoming bolder, overthrew the one and the other monarchy.

The portrait painted of Tarquin is not flattering; his name did not escape any of the orators who had something to say against tyranny. But his conduct before his misfortune —which we know he himself foresaw, his mild treatment of conquered peoples, his generosity toward the soldiers, the art he had of interesting so many people in his preservation, his public works, his courage in war, his constancy in misfortune, a war that he waged or had waged against the Roman people for twenty years when he had neither realm nor wealth, his continual resourcefulness—all clearly show that he was not a contemptible man.

The places bestowed by posterity are subject, like others, to the caprice of fortune. Woe to the reputation of any prince who is oppressed by a party that becomes dominant, or who has tried to destroy a prejudice that survives him!

Having ousted the kings, Rome established annual consuls, and this too helped it reach its high degree of power. During their lifetime, princes go through periods of ambition, followed by other passions and by idleness itself. But, with the republic having leaders who changed every year and who sought to signalize their magistracy so that they might obtain new ones, ambition did not lose even a moment. They induced the senate to propose war to the people, and showed it new enemies every day.

This body was already rather inclined that way itself. Wearied incessantly by the complaints and demands of the people, it sought to distract them from their unrest by occupying them abroad.[6]

Now war was almost always agreeable to the people, because, by the wise distribution of booty, the means had been found of making it useful to them.

Since Rome was a city without commerce, and almost without arts, pillage was the only means individuals had of enriching themselves.

The manner of pillaging was therefore brought under control, and it was done with much the same discipline as is now practiced among the inhabitants of Little Tartary.[d]

The booty was assembled [7] and then distributed to the soldiers. None was ever lost, for prior to setting out each man had sworn not to take any for himself. And the Romans were the most religious people in the world when it came to an oath —which always formed the nerve of their military discipline.

Finally, the citizens who remained in the city also enjoyed the fruits of victory. Part of the land of the conquered people was confiscated and divided into two parts. One was sold for public profit, the other distributed to poor citizens subject to a rent paid to the republic.

Since only a conquest or victory could obtain the honor of a triumph for the consuls, they waged war with great impetuosity They went straight for the enemy, and strength decided the matter immediately.

Rome was therefore in an endless and constantly violent war. Now a nation forever at war, and by the very principle of its government, must necessarily do one of two things.

---

[d] Little Tartary: southern Russia, from the Crimea to the Caucasus.

Either it must perish, or it must overcome all the others which were only at war intermittently and were therefore never as ready to attack or as prepared to defend themselves as it was.

In this way the Romans acquired a profound knowledge of military art. In transient wars, most of the examples of conduct are lost; peace brings other ideas, and one's faults and even one's virtues are forgotten.

Another consequence of the principle of continual war was that the Romans never made peace except as victors. In effect, why make a shameful peace with one people to begin attacking another?

With this idea in mind, they always increased their demands in proportion to their defeats. By so doing they consternated their conquerors and imposed on themselves a greater necessity to conquer.

Since they were always exposed to the most frightful acts of vengeance, constancy and valor became necessary to them. And among them these virtues could not be distinguished from the love of oneself, of one's family, of one's country, and of all that is most dear to men.

The peoples of Italy made no use of machines for carrying on sieges.[8] In addition, since the soldiers fought without pay, they could not be retained for long before any one place. Thus, few of their wars were decisive. They fought to pillage the enemy's camp or his lands—after which the victor and vanquished each withdrew to his own city. This is what produced the resistance of the peoples of Italy, and, at the same time, the obstinacy of the Romans in subjugating them. This is what gave the Romans victories which did not corrupt them, and which let them remain poor.

If they had rapidly conquered all the neighboring cities, they would have been in decline at the arrival of Pyrrhus, the Gauls, and Hannibal. And following the fate of nearly all the states in the world, they would have passed too quickly from poverty to riches, and from riches to corruption.

But, always striving and always meeting obstacles, Rome made its power felt without being able to extend it, and, within a very small orbit, practiced the virtues which were to be so fatal to the world.

All the peoples of Italy were not equally warlike. The Tuscans had grown soft from their affluence and luxury. The Tarentines, Capuans, and nearly all the cities of Campania and Magna Graecia[e] languished in idleness and pleasures. But the Latins, Hernicans, Sabines, Aequians, and Volscians loved war passionately. They were all around Rome. Their resistance to it was unbelievable, and they outdid it in obstinacy.

The Latin cities were colonies of Alba founded [9] by Latinus Sylvius. Aside from a common origin with the Romans, they also had common rites, and Servius Tullius [10] had induced them to build a temple in Rome to serve as the center of the union of the two peoples. Having lost a great battle near Lake Regillus, they were subjected to an alliance and military association [11] with the Romans.

During the short time the tyranny of the decemvirs lasted, we clearly see the degree to which the extension of Rome's power depended on its liberty. The state seemed to have lost [12] the soul which animated it.

There were then only two sorts of men in the city: those who endured servitude, and those who sought to impose it for their own interests. The senators withdrew from Rome as from a foreign city, and the neighboring peoples met with no resistance anywhere.

---

[e] Campania: a district of western Italy below Latium; Magna Graecia: southern Italy, where there were numerous colonies founded by the Greeks.

When the senate had the means of paying the soldiers, the siege of Veii was undertaken. It lasted ten years. The Romans employed a new art and a new way of waging war. Their successes were more brilliant; they profited more from their victories; they made larger conquests; they sent out more colonies. In short, the taking of Veii was a kind of revolution.

But their labors were not lessened. The very fact that they struck harder blows against the Tuscans, Aequians, and Volscians caused their allies—the Latins and Hernicans, who had the same arms and discipline they did—to abandon them. It caused the Samnites, the most warlike of all the peoples of Italy, to wage war against them furiously.

With the establishment of military pay, the senate no longer distributed the lands of conquered peoples to the soldiers. It imposed other conditions on these peoples; it required them, for example, to furnish [13] the army with its pay for a certain time, and to give it grain and clothing.

The capture of Rome by the Gauls deprived it of none of its strength. Dispersed rather than vanquished, almost the whole army withdrew to Veii. The people took refuge in the neighboring cities; and the burning of the city only amounted to the burning of some shepherds' cabins.

NOTES

1. See the amazement of Dionysius of Halicarnassus at the sewers built by Tarquin; *Roman Antiquities,* III (67). They still exist.
2. Plutarch, *Life of Romulus* (21).
3. This is shown by the whole history of the kings of Rome.
4. The senate named a magistrate of the interregnum who elected the king; this election had to be confirmed by the people. See Dionysius of Halicarnassus, II (40), III, and IV.
5. See Zonaras (VII, 9) and Dionysius of Halicarnassus, IV (43).

6. Besides, the authority of the senate was less limited in external affairs than in those of the city.
7. See Polybius, X (16).
8. Dionysius of Halicarnassus, IX (68), says so expressly, and it is shown by history. They did not know how to make galleries to shelter themselves from the besieged; they tried to take cities by scaling the walls. Ephorus recorded that Artemon, an engineer, invented heavy machines for battering down the strongest walls. Pericles used them first at the siege of Samos, according to Plutarch's *Life of Pericles* (27).
9. As we see in the treatise entitled *Origin of the Roman People* (17), believed to be by Aurelius Victor.
10. Dionysius of Halicarnassus, IV (26).
11. See one of the treaties made with them, in Dionysius of Halicarnassus, VI (115).
12. On the pretext of giving the people written laws, they seized the government. See Dionysius of Halicarnassus, XI.
13. See the treaties that were made.

CHAPTER II

THE ART OF WAR AMONG
THE ROMANS

Destined for war, and regarding it as the only art, the Romans put their whole spirit and all their thoughts into perfecting it. It was doubtlessly a god, says Vegetius,[1] who inspired them with the idea of the legion.

They judged it necessary to give the soldiers of the legion offensive and defensive arms stronger and heavier [2] than those of any other people.

But since warfare requires things that a heavy troop cannot do, they wanted the legion to contain in its midst a light troop that could sally forth into battle, and, if necessary, withdraw to it. They also wanted the legion to have cavalry, archers,[a] and slingers to pursue fugitives and consummate the victory. They wanted it to be defended by every type of war machinery, drawn along with it. They wanted it to entrench every evening and become, as Vegetius [3] says, a kind of fortress.

So that they could handle heavier arms than other men, they had to make themselves more than men. This they did by continual labor, which increased their strength, and by

---

[a] The term translated as "archers" is *hommes de trait* and actually refers to soldiers who shot or hurled various kinds of missiles.

exercises giving them dexterity, which is nothing more than the proper use of one's strength.

We observe today that our armies suffer great losses from the soldiers laboring [4] excessively, yet it was by enormous labor that the Romans preserved themselves. The reason is, I believe, that their toil was continual, whereas our soldiers constantly go from extremes of labor to extremes of idleness— which is the best way in the world to destroy them.

I must report here what the authors [5] tell us about the education of Roman soldiers. They were accustomed to marching at military pace, that is, to covering twenty miles, and sometimes twenty-four, in five hours. During these marches, they had to carry sixty-pound packs. They were kept in the habit of running and jumping completely armed. In their exercises they used [6] swords, javelins, and arrows double the weight of ordinary arms, and these exercises were continual.

The camp was not their only military school. There was a place in the city where citizens went to exercise (the Campus Martius). After their labors,[7] they threw themselves into the Tiber to keep up their swimming ability and clean off the dust and sweat.

We no longer have the right idea about physical exercises. A man who applies himself to them excessively seems contemptible to us because their only purpose now is enjoyment. For the ancients, however, all exercises, including the dance, were part of the military art.

With us it has even come to pass that too studied a dexterity in the use of military weapons has become ridiculous. For since the introduction of the custom of single combat, fencing has come to be regarded as the science of quarrelers or cowards.

Those who criticize Homer for usually exalting the physical strength, dexterity or agility of his heroes should find Sallust quite ridiculous when he praises Pompey [8] "for running, jumping and carrying a load as well as any man of his time."

Whenever the Romans believed themselves in danger or wanted to make up for some loss, their usual practice was to tighten military discipline. Is it necessary to wage war against the Latins—peoples as inured to war as themselves? Manlius, intent on strengthening his authority, has his own son put to death for conquering the enemy without an order to do so. Are they defeated at Numantia? Scipio Aemilianus immediately deprives them of everything that had made them soft.[9] Have the Roman legions been forced to submit in Numidia? Metellus repairs this shame as soon as he has made them revive their old institutions. To defeat the Cimbri and the Teutones, Marius begins by turning rivers from their course. And when the soldiers of Sulla's army are afraid of the war against Mithridates, he works them so hard [10] that they beg for combat as an end to their pains.

Publius Nasica made them construct a fleet without needing one. Idleness was feared more than their enemies.

Aulus Gellius [11,b] gives rather poor reasons for the Roman custom of bleeding soldiers who had committed some offense. The true reason is that weakening them was a means of degrading them, since strength is a soldier's main attribute.

Men so hardened were in general healthy. We do not notice in the authors that the Roman armies, which made war in so many climates, lost many men through sickness. But today it happens almost continually that armies dissolve, so to speak, in a campaign without fighting a single battle.

Among us desertions are frequent because soldiers are the vilest part of each nation, and no one nation has or believes it has an unquestionable advantage over the others. With the Romans they were more rare. Soldiers drawn from

---

[b] Aulus Gellius was a Latin author and grammarian (c. 130-180 A.D.).

the midst of a people that was so bold, so proud, so sure of commanding others could scarcely think of humbling themselves to the point of ceasing to be Romans.

Since their armies were not large,[c] it was easy to provide for their subsistence. The commander could know them better, and detected offenses and breaches of discipline more easily.

The strength they derived from their exercises and the admirable roads they had constructed enabled them to make long and rapid marches.[12] Their unexpected appearance chilled the spirit. They showed up particularly after a setback, when their enemies were displaying the negligence that usually follows victory.

In our battles today, an individual soldier hardly has any confidence except when he is part of a multitude. But each Roman, more robust and inured to war than his opponent, always relied on himself. Courage—the virtue which is the consciousness of one's own strength—came to him naturally.

Since their troops were always the best disciplined, it was unusual, even in the most unfavorable battle, if they did not rally somewhere, or if disorder did not arise somewhere among their opponents. The histories, therefore, constantly show them wresting victory from the hands of the enemy in the end, although at first they may have been overcome by his numbers or his ardor.

Their chief care was to examine in what way the enemy might be superior to them, and they corrected the defect immediately. They became accustomed to seeing blood and wounds at their gladiatorial exhibitions, which they acquired from the Etruscans.[13]

The cutting swords[14] of the Gauls and the elephants of Pyrrhus surprised them only once. They made up for

---

[c] An army, consisting of two legions, had about twelve thousand Romans in it and an equal number of allies.

the weakness of their cavalry,[15] first by removing the bridles
of their horses so that their impetuosity could not be restrained, then by introducing velites.[16] When they became
familiar with the Spanish sword,[17] they abandoned their own.
They got around the skill of pilots by inventing a device
Polybius describes to us.[d] In sum, as Josephus says,[18] war was
a meditation for them, and peace an exercise.

If nature or its institutions gave a nation some particular
advantage, the Romans immediately made use of it. They
left no stone unturned to get Numidian horses, Cretan archers,
Balearic slingers, and Rhodian vessels.

In short, no nation ever prepared for war with so much
prudence, or waged it with so much audacity.

NOTES

1. II, 1 (II, 21).
2. See what the arms of the Roman soldier were in Polybius
   (VI, 21) and in Josephus, *The Jewish War*, II (III, 5, 6).
   The latter says there is little difference between packhorses
   and Roman soldiers. "They carry," Cicero tells us, "food
   for more than fifteen days, everything they will use, and
   whatever is necessary to fortify themselves. As for their
   arms, they are no more encumbered by them than by their hands."
   Tusculan Disputations, III (II, 16).
3. II, 25.
4. Especially from digging up the ground.
5. See Vegetius, I (9). See in Livy, XXVI (51), the exercises
   Scipio Africanus made his soldiers do after the capture of
   New Carthage. Marius, in spite of his old age, went to the
   Campus Martius every day. Pompey, at the age of fifty-eight,
   went in full armor to fight with the young men; he mounted
   his horse, rode at full speed, and hurled his javelins. Plutarch,
   Lives of Marius and Pompey.

---

[d] Polybius, I, 22.

6. Vegetius, I (11-14).
7. Vegetius I (10).
8. *Cum alacribus saltu, cum velocibus cursu, cum validis vecte certabat.* (He vied in leaping with the most active, in running with the swiftest, and in exercises of strength with the most robust). Fragment of Sallust, reported by Vegetius, I, 9.
9. He sold all the beasts of burden of the army, and made each soldier carry thirty days of grain and seven stakes. Florus, *Epitome*, LVII.
10. Frontinus, *Strategems*, I, 11.
11. X, 8.
12. See especially the defeat of Hasdrubal and their diligence against Viriathus.
13. Fragment of Nicolaus of Damascus, X, taken from Athenaeus, IV (39). Before the soldiers left for the army, they were shown a gladiatorial combat. Julius Capitolinus, *Lives of Maximus and Balbinus.*
14. The Romans held out their javelins, which received the strokes of the Gallic swords, and blunted them.
15. Nevertheless, it was better than the cavalry of the small peoples of Italy. It was formed from the leading citizens, for each of whom a horse was maintained at public expense. When dismounted, there was no more redoubtable infantry, and very often it was decisive in achieving victory.
16. These were young men, lightly armed, and the most agile in the legion, who, at the slightest signal, jumped on the rump of the horses, or fought on foot. Valerius Maximus, II (3); Livy, XXVI (4).
17. Fragment of Polybius cited by Suidas in connection with the word μάχαιρα.
18. *The Jewish War*, II (III, 5, 6).

CHAPTER III

HOW THE ROMANS WERE ABLE

TO EXPAND

Since all the peoples of Europe these days have practically the same arts, the same arms, the same discipline, and the same way of making war, the marvelous good fortune of the Romans seems incredible to us. Besides, such great differences in power exist today that a small state cannot possibly rise by its own efforts from the lowly position in which Providence has placed it.

This calls for reflection; otherwise, we would see events without understanding them, and, by not being aware of the difference in situations, would believe that the men we read about in ancient history are of another breed than ourselves.

In Europe constant experience has shown that a prince who has a million subjects cannot maintain more than ten thousand troops without ruining himself. Only great nations therefore have armies.

It was not the same in the ancient republics. Today the proportion of soldiers to the rest of the people is one to a hundred, whereas with them it could easily be one to eight.

The founders of the ancient republics had made an equal partition of the lands. This alone produced a powerful people, that is, a well-regulated society. It also produced a good army, everyone having an equal, and very great, interest in defending his country.

When the laws were no longer stringently observed, a situation just like the one we are in came about. The avarice of some individuals and the prodigality of others caused landed property to pass into the hands of a few, and the arts were at once introduced for the mutual needs of rich and poor. As a result, almost no citizens or soldiers were left. Landed properties previously destined for their support were employed for the support of slaves and artisans—instruments of the luxury of the new owners. And without this the state, which had to endure in spite of its disorder, would have perished. Before the corruption set in, the primary incomes of the state were divided among the soldiers, that is, the farmers. When the republic was corrupt, they passed at once to rich men, who gave them back to the slaves and artisans. And by means of taxes a part was taken away for the support of the soldiers.

Now men like these were scarcely fit for war. They were cowardly, and already corrupted by the luxury of the cities, and often by their craft itself. Besides, since they had no country in the proper sense of the term, and could pursue their trade anywhere, they had little to lose or to preserve.

In a census of Rome [1] taken some time after the expulsion of the kings, and in the one Demetrius of Phalerum took at Athens,[2] nearly the same number of inhabitants was found. Rome had a population of four hundred and forty thousand, Athens four hundred and thirty-one thousand. But this census of Rome came at a time when its institutions were vigorous, and that of Athens at a time when it was entirely corrupt. It was discovered that the number of citizens at the age of puberty constituted one fourth of Rome's inhabitants and a little less than one twentieth of Athens'. At these different times, therefore, the power of Rome was to the power of Athens nearly as one quarter to one twentieth—that is, it was five times larger.

When the kings Agis and Cleomenes realized that instead

of the nine thousand citizens Sparta had in Lycurgus' time,[3] only seven hundred were left, hardly a hundred of whom were landowners,[4] and that the rest were only a mob of cowards, they set out to restore the laws[5] in this regard. Lacedaemon regained the power it once had and again became formidable to all the Greeks.

It was the equal partition of lands that at first enabled Rome to rise from its lowly position; and this was obvious when it became corrupt.

It was a small republic when, after the Latins refused to contribute the troops they had promised, ten legions were raised in the city on the spot.[6] "Today's Rome," says Livy, "even though the whole world cannot contain it, could hardly do as much if an enemy suddenly appeared before its walls. This is a certain indication that we have not become greater at all, and that we have only increased the luxury and riches that obsess us."

"Tell me," said Tiberius Gracchus to the nobles,[7] "who is worth more: a citizen or a perpetual slave; a soldier, or a man useless for war? In order to have a few more acres of land than other citizens, do you wish to renounce the hope of conquering the rest of the world, or to place yourself in danger of seeing these lands you refuse us snatched away by enemies?"

NOTES

1. This is the census of which Dionysius of Halicarnassus speaks in IX, art. 25, and which seems to me to be the same as the one he reports toward the end of his sixth book, which was taken sixteen years after the expulsion of the kings.
2. Ctesicles, in Athenaeus, VI.
3. These were citizens of the city, properly called Spartans. Lycurgus made nine thousand shares for them; he gave thirty thousand to the other inhabitants. See Plutarch. *Life of Lycurgus* (8).

4. See Plutarch, *Lives of Agis and Cleomenes*.

5. *Ibid.*

6. Livy, First Decade, VII (25). This was some time after the capture of Rome, under the consulate of L. Furius Camillus and Ap. Claudius Crassus.

7. Appian, *The Civil War* (I, 11).

CHAPTER IV

1. THE GAULS

2. PYRRHUS

3. COMPARISON OF CARTHAGE AND ROME

4. HANNIBAL'S WAR

The Romans had many wars with the Gauls. The love of glory, the contempt for death, and the stubborn will to conquer were the same in the two peoples. But their arms were different. The buckler of the Gauls was small, and their sword poor. They were therefore treated in much the same way as the Mexicans were treated by the Spaniards in recent centuries. And the surprising thing is that these peoples, whom the Romans met in almost all places, and at almost all times, permitted themselves to be destroyed one after the other without ever knowing, seeking or forestalling the cause of their misfortunes.

Pyrrhus came to make war on the Romans at a time when they were in a position to resist him and to learn from his victories. He taught them to entrench, and to choose and arrange a camp. He accustomed them to elephants and prepared them for greater wars.

Pyrrhus' greatness consisted only in his personal qualities.[1] Plutarch tells us that he was forced to undertake the Macedonian war because he could not support the eight thousand infantry and five hundred cavalry that he had.[2] This prince— ruler of a small state of which nothing was heard after him— was an adventurer who constantly undertook new enterprises because he could exist only while undertaking them.

His allies, the Tarentines, had strayed far from the institutions of their ancestors,[3] the Lacedaemonians. He could have done great things with the Samnites, but the Romans had all but destroyed them.

Having become rich sooner than Rome, Carthage had also been corrupted sooner. In Rome, public office could be obtained only through virtue, and brought with it no benefit other than honor and being preferred for further toils, while in Carthage everything the public could give to individuals was for sale, and all service rendered by individuals was paid for by the public.

The tyranny of a prince does no more to ruin a state than does indifference to the common good to ruin a republic. The advantage of a free state is that revenues are better administered in it. But what if they are more poorly administered? The advantage of a free state is that there are no favorites in it. But when that is not the case—when it is necessary to line the pockets of the friends and relatives, not of a prince, but of all those who participate in the government—all is lost. There is greater danger in the laws being evaded in a free state than in their being violated by a prince, for a prince is always the foremost citizen of his state, and has more interest in preserving it than anyone else.

The old morals, a certain custom favoring poverty, made

fortunes at Rome nearly equal, but at Carthage individuals had the riches of kings.

Of the two factions that ruled in Carthage, one always wanted peace, the other war, so that it was impossible there to enjoy the former or do well at the latter.

While war at once united all interests in Rome, it separated them still further in Carthage.[4]

In states governed by a prince, dissensions are easily pacified because he has in his hands a coercive power that brings the two parties together. But in a republic they are more durable, because the evil usually attacks the very power that could cure it.

In Rome, governed by laws, the people allowed the senate to direct public affairs. In Carthage, governed by abuses, the people wanted to do everything themselves.

Carthage, which made war against Roman poverty with its opulence, was at a disadvantage by that very fact. Gold and silver are exhausted, but virtue, constancy, strength and poverty never are.

The Romans were ambitious from pride, the Carthaginians from avarice; the Romans wanted to command, the Carthaginians to acquire. Constantly calculating receipts and expenses, the latter always made war without loving it.

Lost battles, the decrease in population, the enfeeblement of commerce, the exhaustion of the public treasury, the revolt of neighboring nations could make Carthage accept the most severe conditions of peace. But Rome was not guided by experiences of goods and evils. Only its glory determined its actions, and since it could not imagine itself existing without commanding, no hope or fear could induce it to make a peace it did not impose.

There is nothing so powerful as a republic in which the laws are observed not through fear, not through reason, but through passion—which was the case with Rome and Lacedaemon. For then all the strength a faction could have is joined to the wisdom of a good government.

The Carthaginians used foreign troops, and the Romans employed their own. Since the latter never regarded the vanquished as anything but instruments for further triumphs, they made soldiers of all the peoples they had overcome, and the more trouble they had in conquering them, the more they judged them suitable for incorporation into their republic. Thus we see the Samnites, who were subjugated only after twenty-four triumphs,[5] become the auxiliaries of the Romans. And some time before the Second Punic War they drew from them and their allies—that is, from a country scarcely larger than the states of the pope and of Naples—seven hundred thousand infantry and seventy thousand cavalry to oppose the Gauls.[6]

At the height of the Second Punic War, Rome always had from twenty-two to twenty-four legions in action. Yet it appears from Livy that the census then indicated only about one hundred and thirty-seven thousand citizens.

Carthage employed greater forces for attacking, Rome for defending itself. The latter, as has just been said, armed a prodigious number of men against the Gauls and Hannibal, who attacked it, and sent out only two legions against the greatest kings—a policy which perpetuated its forces.

Carthage's situation at home was less secure than Rome's. Rome had thirty colonies around it, which were like ramparts.[7] Prior to the battle of Cannae, no ally had abandoned it, for the Samnites and the other peoples of Italy were accustomed to its domination.

Since most of the cities of Africa were lightly fortified, they surrendered at once to whoever came to take them. Thus, all who disembarked there—Agathocles, Regulus, Scipio—immediately drove Carthage to despair.

The ills which befell the Carthaginians throughout the

war waged against them by the first Scipio can only be attributed to a bad government. Their city and even their armies
were starving, while the Romans had an abundance of all
things.[8]

Among the Carthaginians, armies which had been defeated
became more insolent. Sometimes they crucified their generals,
and punished them for their own cowardice. Among the
Romans, the consul decimated the troops that had fled, and
led them back against the enemy.

The rule of the Carthaginians was very harsh.[9] So severely
had they tormented the peoples of Spain that when the
Romans arrived there they were regarded as liberators. And,
if we bear in mind the immense sums it cost them to support a
war in which they were defeated, we plainly see that injustice
is a bad manager, and that it does not even accomplish its
own ends.

The founding of Alexandria had considerably diminished
the commerce of Carthage. In early times superstition practically banished foreigners from Egypt, and, when the Persians conquered it, they had thought only of weakening their
new subjects. But under the Greek kings Egypt carried on
almost all the commerce of the world, and that of Carthage
began to decline.

Commercial powers can continue in a state of mediocrity
a long time, but their greatness is of short duration. They rise
little by little, without anyone noticing, for they engage in no
particular action that resounds and signals their power. But
when things have come to the point where people cannot help
but see what has happened, everyone seeks to deprive this
nation of an advantage it has obtained, so to speak, only by
surprise.

The Carthaginian cavalry was superior to the Roman for
two reasons. First, the Numidian and Spanish horses were
better than those of Italy; second, the Roman cavalry was

poorly armed, for it was only during the wars the Romans fought in Greece that this feature was changed, as we learn from Polybius.[10]

In the First Punic War, Regulus was beaten as soon as the Carthaginians chose to bring their cavalry into combat on the plains, and, in the Second, Hannibal owed his principal victories to his Numidians.[11]

After Scipio conquered Spain and made an alliance with Masinissa, he took this superiority away from the Carthaginians. It was the Numidian cavalry that won the battle of Zama and finished the war.

The Carthaginians had more experience on the sea and could manoeuver better than the Romans, but I think this advantage was not so great then as it would be today.

Since the ancients did not have the compass, they could hardly navigate anywhere but near the coasts. Also, they used only boats with oars, which were small and flat. Practically every inlet was a harbor for them. The skill of pilots was very limited, and their manoeuvers amounted to very little. Thus Aristotle said [12] that it was useless to have a corps of sailors, and that laborers sufficed for the job.

The art was so imperfect that they could scarcely do with a thousand oars what today is done with a hundred.[13]

Large vessels were disadvantageous, since the difficulty the crew had in moving them made them unable to execute the necessary turns. Anthony had a disastrous experience [14] with them at Actium; his ships could not move, while Augustus' lighter ones attacked them on all sides.

Because ancient vessels were rowed, the lighter ones easily shattered the oars of the larger ones, which then became nothing more than immobile objects, like our dismasted vessels today.

Since the invention of the compass, things have changed. Oars have been abandoned,[15] the coasts have been left behind, great vessels have been built. The ship has become more complicated, and sailing practices have multiplied.

The invention of powder had an unsuspected effect. It made the strength of navies consist more than ever in nautical art. For to resist the cannon's violence and avoid being subjected to superior firing power, great ships were needed. But the level of the art had to correspond to the magnitude of the ship.

The small vessels of former days used to grapple on to each other suddenly, and the soldiers of both sides did the fighting. A whole land army was placed on a fleet. In the naval battle that Regulus and his colleague won, we see one hundred and thirty thousand Romans fighting against one hundred and fifty thousand Carthaginians. At that time soldiers meant a great deal and an expert crew little; at present, soldiers mean nothing, or little, and an expert crew a great deal.

The victory of the consul Duilius brings out this difference well. The Romans had no knowledge of navigation. A Carthaginian galley ran aground on their coasts; they used it as a model to build their own. In three months' time, their sailors were trained, their fleet constructed and equipped. It put to sea, found the Carthaginian navy and defeated it.

At present, a lifetime hardly suffices for a prince to create a fleet capable of appearing before a power which already rules the sea. It is perhaps the only thing that money alone cannot do. And if, in our day, a great prince immediately succeeds at it,[16] others have learned from experience that his example is more to be admired than followed.[17]

The Second Punic War is so famous that everybody knows it. When we carefully examine the multitude of obstacles confronting Hannibal, all of which this extraordinary man surmounted, we have before us the finest spectacle presented by antiquity.

Rome was a marvel of constancy. After the battles of Ticinus, Trebia, and Lake Trasimene, after Cannae more dismal still, abandoned by almost all the peoples of Italy, it did not sue for peace. The reason is that the senate never departed from its old maxims.[a] It dealt with Hannibal as it had previously dealt with Pyrrhus, with whom it had refused to make any accommodation so long as he remained in Italy. And I find in Dionysius of Halicarnassus [18] that, at the time of the negotiation with Coriolanus, the senate declared that it would not violate its old practices, that the Roman people could not make peace while enemies were on its soil, but that, if the Volscians withdrew, their just demands would be met.

Rome was saved by the strength of its institutions. After the battle of Cannae not even the women were permitted to shed tears. The senate refused to ransom the prisoners, and sent the miserable remains of the army to make war in Sicily, without pay or any military honor, until such time as Hannibal was expelled from Italy.

In another instance, the consul Terentius Varro had fled shamefully to Venusia.[b] This man, who was of the lowest birth, had been elevated to the consulate only to mortify the nobility. But the senate did not wish to enjoy this unhappy triumph. Seeing how necessary it was on this occasion to win the confidence of the people, it went before Varro and thanked him for not having despaired of the republic.

Usually it is not the real loss sustained in battle (such as that of several thousands of men) which proves fatal to a

---

[a] The French word *maxime* means "rule of conduct"; "maxim," in English, still has this as one of its meanings, and, for the sake of simplicity and consistency, will be used throughout.

[b] Venusia: an Italian city of Apulia, some distance south of Rome.

state, but the imagined loss and the discouragement, which deprive it of the very strength fortune had left it.

There are things that everybody says because they were once said.[c] People believe that Hannibal made a signal error in not having laid siege to Rome after the battle of Cannae. It is true that at first the terror in Rome was extreme, but the consternation of a warlike people, which almost always turns into courage, is different from that of a vile populace, which senses only its weakness. A proof that Hannibal would not have succeeded is that the Romans were still able to send assistance everywhere.

People say further that Hannibal made a great mistake in leading his army to Capua, where it grew soft. But they fail to see that they stop short of the true cause. Would not the soldiers of his army have found Capua everywhere, having become rich after so many victories? On a similar occasion, Alexander, who was commanding his own subjects, made use of an expedient that Hannibal, who had only mercenary troops, could not use. He had the baggage of his soldiers set on fire, and burned all their riches and his too. We are told that Kuli Khan,[d] after his conquest of India, left each soldier with only a hundred rupees of silver.[19]

It was Hannibal's conquests themselves that began to change the fortunes of this war. He had not been sent to Italy by the magistrates of Carthage; he received very little help, whether because of the jealousy of one party or the overconfidence of the other. While he retained his whole army, he defeated the Romans. But when he had to put garrisons in the cities, defend his allies, besiege strongholds or prevent

---

[c] For this reference and the one in the next paragraph, see Livy, XXII, 51, and XXIII, 18.

[d] Kuli Khan: Nadir Shah, who was shah of Iran from 1736-47. A.D.

them from being besieged, his forces were found to be too small, and he lost a large part of his army piecemeal. Conquests are easy to make, because they are made with all one's forces; they are difficult to preserve because they are defended with only a part of one's forces.

NOTES

1. See a fragment from Dio, I, in *The Extract of Virtues and Vices*.
2. *Life of Pyrrhus* (26).
3. Justin, XX (1).
4. The presence of Hannibal made all dissensions among the Romans cease, but Scipio's presence embittered the dissensions already existing among the Carthaginians, and took all the remaining strength from the government. The generals, the senate, the notables became more suspect to the people, and the people became wilder. See, in Appian, the entire war of the first Scipio.
5. Florus, I (16).
6. See Polybius (II, 24). Florus' *Epitome* says that they raised three hundred thousand men in the city and among the Latins.
7. Livy, XXVII (9, 10).
8. See Appian, *The Punic Wars* (25).
9. See what Polybius says of their exactions, especially in the fragment of book IX (11) in *The Extract of Virtues and Vices*.
10. VI (25).
11. Entire corps of Numidians went over to the side of the Romans, who from that point began to breathe again.
12. *Politics*, VII (6 (5).
13. See what Perrault says about the oars of the ancients, *Essay in Physics*, tit. III, *Mechanics of the Ancients*.
14. The same thing happened at the battle of Salamis. Plutarch, *Life of Themistocles* (14). History is full of similar facts.

15. From which we can judge the imperfection of the navigation of the ancients, since we have abandoned a practice in which we were so superior to them.
16. Louis XIV.
17. Spain and Muscovy.
18. *Roman Antiquities,* VIII.
19. *History of His Life,* Paris, 1742, p. 402.

CHAPTER V

THE CONDITION OF GREECE, MACEDONIA, SYRIA, AND EGYPT AFTER THE REDUCTION OF THE CARTHAGINIANS

I imagine Hannibal made few witty remarks and even fewer favoring Fabius and Marcellus over himself.[a] I regret seeing Livy strewing his flowers on these enormous colosses of antiquity. I wish he had done as Homer, who refrained from adorning them and knew so well how to make them come alive.

Furthermore, the remarks attributed to Hannibal should be sensible. For if on learning of his brother's defeat he confessed he foresaw the ruin of Carthage, I know nothing better calculated to throw despair into the peoples who had placed themselves under his protection, and to discourage an army which expected such great rewards after the war.

Since the Carthaginians faced only victorious armies in Spain, Sicily, and Sardinia, Hannibal—whose enemies were constantly gaining strength—was reduced to a defensive war.

---

[a] For the passages referred to here and in the next paragraph, see Livy, XXVII, 16, 51.

This gave the Romans the idea of carrying the war to Africa, and Scipio went there. The successes he had there forced the Carthaginians to recall Hannibal from Italy, weeping for grief as he yielded to the Romans the soil on which he had vanquished them so often.

Everything a great statesman and captain can do, Hannibal did to save his country. Unable to induce Scipio to make peace, he fought a battle in which fortune seemed to take pleasure in confounding his skill, experience, and good sense.

Carthage obtained peace not from an enemy but from a master. It was forced to pay ten thousand talents in fifty years, to give hostages, to hand over its vessels and elephants, and to make no war without the consent of the Roman people. And the power of its inveterate enemy, Masinissa, was increased in order to keep it humbled forever.

After the reduction of the Carthaginians, Rome had almost nothing but small wars and great victories, whereas before it had had small victories and great wars.

In those times something like two separate worlds existed. In one, the Carthaginians and Romans fought each other. The other was agitated by quarrels dating from Alexander's death. There no thought was given to what was happening in the West,[1] for although Philip, king of Macedonia, had made a treaty with Hannibal, it was practically without consequence. And this prince, who gave the Carthaginians nothing but very feeble assistance, only demonstrated useless ill will toward the Romans.

When we see two great peoples engage in a long and stubborn war, it is often impolitic to think we can remain tranquil spectators. For the people which wins immediately undertakes new wars, and a nation of soldiers goes off to fight against peoples who are only citizens.

This was shown very clearly in those times, for the Romans had hardly subdued the Carthaginians when they attacked new peoples and appeared everywhere on earth to invade every country.

Only four powers in the East were then capable of resisting the Romans: Greece, and the kingdoms of Macedonia, Syria, and Egypt. Let us see what the situation of these first two powers was, since the Romans began by subjugating them.

Three notable peoples lived in Greece: the Aetolians, the Achaeans, and the Boeotians. These were grouped in associations of free cities which had general assemblies and common magistrates. The Aetolians were warlike, hardy, reckless, greedy for gain, and always free with their word and oaths; in short, they made war on land as pirates do at sea. The Achaeans were constantly vexed by troublesome neighbors or protectors. The Boeotians, dullest of the Greeks, participated as little as possible in general affairs. Led solely by their immediate experience of good and evil, they did not have enough spirit to make it easy for orators to agitate them, and, surprisingly, their republic was preserved amid anarchy itself.[2]

Lacedaemon had preserved its power—that is, the warlike spirit with which the institutions of Lycurgus imbued it. The Thessalians were, to a considerable degree, kept in subjection by the Macedonians. The kings of Illyria had already been crushed by the Romans. The Acarnanians and Athamenes [b] were ravaged in turn by the forces of Macedonia and Aetolia. Without any strength of their own and without allies,[3] the Athenians no longer amazed the world except by their flattery of kings. And the tribune where Demosthenes had spoken was no longer mounted except to propose the most cowardly and scandalous decrees.

Otherwise, Greece was formidable because of its situation, its strength, the multitude of its cities, the number of its sol-

---

[b] Acarnanians: a people of western Greece; Athamanes: a people of Epirus.

diers, its public order,[c] its morals, its laws. It loved war, it knew the art of war, and had it been united it would have been invincible.

It had indeed been shaken by the first Philip, Alexander, and Antipater, but not subjugated. And the kings of Macedonia, who could not resolve to abandon their claims and hopes, stubbornly labored to enslave it.

Macedonia was almost surrounded by inaccessible mountains. Its people were admirably suited for war—courageous, obedient, industrious, indefatigable. And they must have received these qualities from the climate, since to this day the men of that country are still the best soldiers of the Turkish empire.

Greece maintained itself by a kind of balance: the Lacedaemonians were usually the allies of the Aetolians, and the Macedonians of the Achaeans. But all equilibrium was upset by the coming of the Romans.

Since the kings of Macedonia could not maintain a great number of troops,[4] the least reverse was of consequence to them. Besides, they would have had trouble extending their power, since their designs were not unknown, and their proceedings were always watched closely. And the successes they had in wars undertaken for their allies were an evil that these same allies sought at once to repair.

But the kings of Macedonia were usually skilful princes. Their monarchy was not one of those that are carried along by a kind of momentum imparted to them at their beginning. Continually instructed by perils and problems, entangled in all the quarrels of the Greeks, they had to win the leaders of

---

c *Police,* the French word here, referred to the function or branch of government involving the keeping of public order and morality—a conception still retained in the "police powers" thought to be inherent in the state governments of the United States. See also Blackstone's *Commentaries,* IV, 13.

the cities, dazzle the peoples, divide or unite interests. In short, they were forced to expose themselves at every moment.

Philip, who at the beginning of his reign won the love and confidence of the Greeks by his moderation, suddenly changed. He became a cruel tyrant, at a time when policy and ambition should have made him just.[5] He saw, though from afar, the Carthaginians and the Romans, whose forces were immense. He had ended the war to the advantage of his allies, and had reconciled himself with the Aetolians. It was natural that he should think of uniting all of Greece behind him in order to prevent foreigners from establishing themselves there. But, instead, he irritated it by small usurpations, and, amusing himself with quarrels about vain interests when his very existence was at stake, he made himself odious and detestable to all the Greeks by three or four bad actions.

The Aetolians were the most irritated, and the Romans, seizing the opportunity offered by their resentment, or rather by their folly, made an alliance with them, entered Greece, and armed it against Philip.

This prince was vanquished at the battle of Cynoscephalae, and the victory was due in part to the valor of the Aetolians. He was so consternated as to be reduced to a treaty that was less a peace than an abandonment of his own forces. He withdrew his garrisons from all Greece, surrendered his vessels, and obligated himself to pay a thousand talents in ten years.

With his usual good sense, Polybius compares the military order of the Romans with that of the Macedonians, which was adopted by all the kings succeeding Alexander. He lets us see the advantages and inconveniences of the phalanx and the legion; he prefers the Roman order, and appears to be right, judging by all the events of those days.

In the Second Punic War, the fact that Hannibal immediately armed his soldiers in Roman style greatly endangered the Romans. But the Greeks changed neither their arms nor their manner of fighting. It did not so much as enter their minds to renounce practices with which they had done such great things.

The success of the Romans against Philip was the greatest of all the steps they took toward general conquest. To assure themselves of Greece, they used all sorts of ways to reduce the Aetolians who had helped them conquer. What is more, they ordained that every Greek city which had been under Philip or some other prince would be governed thenceforth by its own laws.

It is easy to see that these small republics could only be dependent. The Greeks abandoned themselves to senseless delight and believed themselves free in reality because the Romans declared them so.

The Aetolians, who had imagined they would dominate Greece, were in despair upon seeing that they had only succeeded in giving themselves masters. And since they always went to extremes, seeking to correct their follies by still other follies, they called into Greece the king of Syria, Antiochus, as they had called in the Romans.

The kings of Syria were the most powerful of Alexander's successors, for they possessed almost all the states of Darius, except Egypt. But events had taken place to weaken their power considerably.

Toward the end of his life, Seleucus, who had founded the Syrian empire, destroyed the kingdom of Lysimachus. In the confusion, several provinces revolted. The kingdoms of Pergamum, Cappadocia, and Bithynia [d] were formed. But these small timid states always regarded the humbling of their old masters as a piece of good fortune for themselves.

Since the kings of Syria always looked upon the felicity of the kingdom of Egypt with extreme envy, they thought of nothing but reconquering it. Neglecting the East for this

---

[d] Pergamum, Cappadocia, and Bithynia were in Asia Minor.

reason, they lost several provinces there and met with much disobedience in the others.

Finally, the kings of Syria held upper and lower Asia,[e] but experience has shown that when the capital and the main forces are in the lower provinces of Asia, the upper ones cannot be preserved, and when the seat of empire is in the upper ones, the state is weakened by the attempt to protect the lower. The Persian and Syrian empires were never as strong as the Parthian, which comprised only a part of the provinces of the other two. If Cyrus had not conquered the kingdom of Lydia, if Seleucus had stayed in Babylonia and had left the maritime provinces to Antigonus' successors, the Persian empire would have been invincible to the Greeks, and Seleucus' to the Romans. Nature has given states certain limits to mortify the ambition of men. When the Romans transgressed these limits, the Parthians almost always destroyed them;[6] when the Parthians dared to transgress them, they were immediately forced to withdraw. And in our own day the Turks, after advancing beyond these limits, were compelled to retire within them.

The kings of Syria and of Egypt had two kinds of subjects in their countries: conquering peoples, and conquered peoples. The former,[f] still thinking of their original condition, were very difficult to govern. They did not have the spirit of independence that prompts men to throw off their yoke, but the impatience that makes them desire to change masters.

But the main weakness of the kingdom of Syria came from that of the court where the successors of Darius and not of Alexander reigned. The luxury, vanity, and indolence which,

---

[e] "Upper" and "lower" Asia, as the terms are used here, refer to the contrast between Iran, on the one hand, and the maritime provinces of Asia Minor, on the other.

[f] Former: This is the wording in Jullian and Masson, yet other editions read "latter."

in all ages, have never left the courts of Asia, reigned especially at this one. The evil passed to the people, and to the soldiers, and became contagious even for the Romans, since the war they waged against Antiochus is the true beginning of their corruption.

Such was the situation of the kingdom of Syria when Antiochus, who had done such great things, undertook to make war against the Romans. But he did not even conduct himself with the prudence one employs in ordinary affairs. Hannibal wanted the war in Italy renewed and Philip won over or made neutral. Antiochus did neither of these. He appeared in Greece with a small part of his forces and, as if he had wanted to observe a war there rather than wage one, he was only concerned with his pleasures. He was defeated and fled to Asia, more frightened than conquered.

In this war, Philip, swept along by the Romans as by a torrent, served them with all his power and became the instrument of their victories. The pleasure of avenging himself and ravaging Aetolia, the promise that his tribute would be reduced and that some cities would be left to him, his jealousy of Antiochus—in short, petty motives—determined his conduct. And, not daring to conceive the idea of throwing off his yoke, he thought only of moderating it.

Antiochus judged matters so badly that he imagined the Romans would leave him alone in Asia. But they followed him there. He was defeated again and, in his consternation, consented to the most infamous treaty a great prince has ever made.

I know nothing so magnanimous as the resolve of a monarch of our own day [7] to be buried under the debris of his throne rather than accept proposals that a king should not even hear. He had too proud a soul to descend lower than the level of his misfortunes, and he well knew that a crown can be strengthened by courage but never by infamy.

It is a common thing to find princes who can conduct a battle. There are very few who know how to wage a war, who are equally capable of taking advantage of fortune and awaiting it, and who, with the frame of mind that makes them cautious before an undertaking, fear nothing once the undertaking is begun.

After the reduction of Antiochus only small powers remained except for Egypt, which by its situation, its fecundity, its commerce, the number of its inhabitants, and its naval and land forces could have been formidable. But the cruelty of its kings, their cowardice, their avarice, their imbecility, their frightful sensuality made them so odious to their subjects that most of the time only the protection of the Romans kept them in power.

It was practically a fundamental law of the crown of Egypt that sisters succeeded to it along with brothers; and, in order to maintain unity in the government, the brother was married to the sister. Now it is difficult to imagine anything in politics more pernicious than such an order of succession. Every little domestic quarrel became a disorder in the state, and whichever one of the pair had the slightest grievance immediately raised the people of Alexandria in revolt against the other. This immense populace was always ready to join the first of its kings who wanted to agitate it. Moreover, since the kingdoms of Cyrene ᵍ and Cyprus were usually in the hands of other princes of this family, all with reciprocal rights of succession, both reigning princes and pretenders to the crown were almost always in existence. These kings therefore sat on an unstable throne, and they were powerless outside the country because they were insecurely established within it.

ᵍ Cyrene: a North African city on the Mediterranean west of Egypt.

The forces of the kings of Egypt, like those of other Asian kings, consisted of their Greek auxiliaries. Aside from the spirit of liberty, honor and glory that animated the Greeks, they were constantly engaged in all sorts of physical exercises. In the main cities they had regular games where the victors obtained crowns in the sight of all Greece, thus producing a general spirit of emulation. Now at a time when arms required strength and dexterity for success in battle, men trained in this way doubtlessly had great advantages over a crowd of barbarians selected at random and led to war involuntarily—as the armies of Darius indeed demonstrated.

To deprive the kings of such a militia and quietly take their main forces from them, the Romans did two things. First, they gradually established it as a maxim among the Greeks that they could not form any alliance, accord help or make war on anyone without Roman consent. In addition, in their treaties with the kings they forbade them to levy troops among the allies of the Romans—which left them only their national troops.[8]

NOTES

1. It is surprising, as Josephus remarks in his book *Against Apion* (I, 12), that neither Herodotus nor Thucydides ever spoke of the Romans, even though they waged such great wars.

2. To please the multitude, the magistrates no longer permitted the courts to open; dying men bequeathed their property to their friends for use at feasts. See a fragment of Polybius, XX (4, 6), in *The Extract of Virtues and Vices*.

3. They had no alliance with the other peoples of Greece. Polybius, VIII (V, 106).

4. See Plutarch, *Life of Flamininus* (2).

5. See, in Polybius (VII, 12), the injustices and cruelties by which Philip discredited himself.

6. I shall speak of the reasons for this in Chapter XV. They are drawn, in part, from the geographic situation of the two empires.
7. Louis XIV.
8. They had already had this policy with the Carthaginians, whom they forced by treaty to make no further use of auxiliary troops, as we see from a fragment of Dio.

CHAPTER VI

THE CONDUCT THE ROMANS

PURSUED TO SUBJUGATE

ALL PEOPLES

In the course of so many successes, when men ordinarily become negligent, the senate always acted with the same profundity; and while the armies caused consternation everywhere, it held on to the nations that had already been struck down.

It set itself up as a tribunal for judging all peoples, and at the end of every war decided the penalties and rewards each had deserved. It took part of the domain of the conquered peoples for Rome's allies, and by this means accomplished two things, attaching to Rome those kings from whom it had little to fear and much to hope for, and weakening others from whom it had little to hope for and everything to fear.

Allies were used to make war on an enemy, but then the destroyers were at once destroyed. Philip was conquered by means of the Aetolians, who immediately afterward were annihilated for having joined with Antiochus. Antiochus was conquered with the help of the Rhodians; but after receiving splendid rewards, they were forever humbled on the pretext of having demanded that peace be made with Persia.

When the Romans had several enemies on their hands they made a truce with the weakest, which believed itself fortunate to obtain it, placing great value on the postponement of its ruin.

While engaging in a great war, the senate pretended not to notice all sorts of wrongs, and waited in silence till the time for punishment had come. And if the people in question sent it the culprits, it refused to punish them, preferring to consider the whole nation criminal and reserving to itself a more useful vengeance.

Since they inflicted unbelievable evils upon their enemies, leagues were hardly ever formed against them, for the country furthest from the peril did not wish to venture closer.

Because of this, they were rarely warred upon, but always went to war at the time, in the manner, and with those that suited them. And of all the peoples they attacked, very few would not have borne all kinds of insults if the Romans had wanted to leave them in peace.

Since it was their custom always to speak as masters, the ambassadors they sent to peoples who had not yet felt their power were sure to be mistreated—which was a sure pretext for waging a new war.[1]

Since they never made peace in good faith, and since universal conquest was their object, their treaties were really only suspensions of war, and they put conditions into them that always began the ruin of the state accepting them. They made garrisons leave strongholds, or limited the number of ground troops, or had horses or elephants surrendered to them. And if the people was a sea power they forced it to burn its vessels and sometimes to live further inland.

After destroying the armies of a prince, they ruined his finances by excessive taxes or a tribute on the pretext of making him pay the expenses of the war—a new kind of tyranny that forced him to oppress his subjects and lose their love.

When they granted peace to some prince, they took one of his brothers or children in hostage, which gave them the means of vexing his kingdom at will. When they had the closest heir, they intimidated the present ruler; if they only had a prince of distant degree, they used him to instigate popular revolts.

When some prince or people broke away from obedience to a ruler, they were immediately accorded the title of ally of the Roman people.[2] This way the Romans made them sacred and inviolable, so that there was no king, however great, who could be sure of his subjects or even of his family for a moment.

Although the title of being their ally entailed a kind of servitude, it was nevertheless much sought after.[3] Those holding it were sure to receive insults only from the Romans, and there were grounds for hoping these would be smaller. Thus, to obtain it there were no services peoples and kings were not ready to render, and no baseness to which they would not stoop.

They had many sorts of allies. Some were united to them by privileges and a participation in their greatness, like the Latins and Hernicans; others, by origin itself, like their colonies; some by benefits, as were Masinissa, Eumenes, and Attalus, who received their kingdoms or the extension of their power from the Romans; other by free treaties, and these became subjects through long-existing alliance, like the kings of Egypt, Bithynia, and Cappadocia, and most of the Greek cities; several, finally, by forced treaties, like Philip and Antiochus, for the Romans never made a peace treaty with an enemy unless it contained an alliance—that is, they subjugated no people which did not help them in reducing others.

When they allowed a city to remain free, they immediately caused two factions to arise within it.[4] One upheld local laws and liberty, the other maintained that there was no law except the will of the Romans. And since the latter faction was always the stronger, it is easy to see that such freedom was only a name.

Sometimes they became masters of a country on the pretext of succession. They entered Asia, Bithynia, and Libya by the testaments of Attalus, Nicomedes,[5] and Apion,[a] and Egypt was enslaved by the testament of the king of Cyrene.

To keep great princes permanently weak, the Romans did not want them to make any alliance with those to whom they had accorded their own.[6] And since they did not refuse their own to a powerful prince's neighbors, this condition, stipulated in a peace treaty, left him without allies.

Moreover, when they had conquered some eminent prince, they wrote into the treaty that he could not have recourse to war to settle his differences with allies of the Romans (that is, usually with all his neighbors), but that he would have to use arbitration. This removed his military power for the future.

And, to reserve all such power to themselves, they deprived even their allies of it. As soon as the allies had the least dispute, the Romans sent ambassadors who forced them to make peace. We need only observe how they terminated the wars of Attalus and Prusias.

When some prince had made a conquest, which often left him exhausted, a Roman ambassador immediately arrived to snatch it from his hands. From among a thousand examples, we can recall how, with a word, they drove Antiochus out of Egypt.

Knowing how well-suited the peoples of Europe were for war, they made it a law that no Asian king would be permitted to enter Europe and subjugate any people whatsoever.[7] The main motive for their war against Mithridates was that

---

[a] Pergamum is said to have been willed to the Romans by Attalus III (133 B.C.), Bithynia by Nicomedes III (74 B.C.), and Cyrene by Apion (96 B.C.).

he had contravened this prohibition by subduing some barbarians.[8]

When they saw two peoples at war, even though they had no alliance or dispute with one or the other, they never failed to appear on the scene. And like our knights-errant, they took the part of the weaker. Dionysius of Halicarnassus [9] says it was an old practice of the Romans always to extend their help to whomever came to implore it.

These practices of the Romans were in no sense just particular actions occurring by chance. These were ever-constant principles, as may readily be seen from the fact that the maxims they followed against the greatest powers were precisely the ones they had followed, in the beginning, against the small cities around them.

They used Eumenes and Masinissa to subjugate Philip and Antiochus in the same way they had used the Latins and Hernicans to subjugate the Volscians and Tuscans. They required the fleets of Carthage and of the Asian kings to be surrendered to them in the same way that they had forced the barks of Antium to be given up. They removed the political and civil links connecting the four parts of Macedonia in the same way that they had formerly broken up the union of the small Latin cities.[10]

But, above all, their constant maxim was to divide. The Achaean republic was formed by an association of free cities. The senate declared that thenceforth each city would be governed by its own laws, without depending on a common authority.

The republic of the Boeotians was similarly a league of several cities. But in the war against Perseus some cities sided with Perseus and the rest with the Romans, and the Romans took the latter into their favor only on condition that the common alliance be dissolved.

If a great prince [b] who reigned in our day had followed

---

[b] This is an allusion to Louis XIV and James II.

these maxims, he would have employed stronger forces to support a neighboring prince who was overthrown by revolt, so as to confine him within the island which remained loyal to him. By dividing the only power that could oppose his designs, he would have derived immense advantages from the very misfortune of his ally.

When disputes broke out in some state, the Romans adjudicated the matter immediately, and by this means they were sure of having against them only the party they had condemned. If princes of the same blood were disputing the crown, the Romans sometimes declared them both kings.[11] If one of them was under age,[12] they decided in his favor and took him under their tutelage, as protectors of the world. For they had carried things to the point where peoples and kings were their subjects without knowing precisely by what title, the rule being that it was enough to have heard of them to owe them submission.

They never waged distant wars without procuring some ally near the enemy under attack, who could join his troops to the army they were sending. And since this army was never very large, they always made sure to keep another [13] in the province nearest the enemy, and a third in Rome constantly ready to march. Thus they exposed only a very small part of their forces, while their enemy hazarded all of his.[14]

Sometimes they abused the subtlety of the terms of their language. They destroyed Carthage, saying that they had promised to preserve the people of the city but not the city itself.[c] We know how the Aetolians, who had entrusted themselves to the good faith of the Romans, were deceived: the Romans claimed that the meaning of the words *to entrust oneself to the good faith of an enemy* [d] entailed the loss of

---

[c] In French the distinction is between *cité* and *ville,* in Latin between *civitas* and *oppidum.*

[d] The Romans interpreted the phrase to mean unconditional surrender. See Jullian, and Polybius, XX, 9.

all sorts of things—of persons, lands, cities, temples, and even tombs.

They could even give a treaty an arbitrary interpretation. Thus, when they wanted to reduce the Rhodians, they said they had not previously given them Lycia as a present but as a friend and ally.

When one of their generals made peace to save his army as it was about to perish, the senate did not ratify the peace but profited from it and continued the war. Thus, when Jugurtha had surrounded a Roman army and, trusting to a treaty, let it go, the very troops he had spared were used against him. And when the Numantians had forced twenty thousand Romans who were about to die of hunger to sue for peace, this peace which had saved so many citizens was broken at Rome, and public faith was evaded by handing back the consul who had signed it.[15]

Sometimes they made peace with a prince on reasonable conditions, and when he had executed them, added such unreasonable ones that he was forced to reopen the war. Thus, after making Jugurtha surrender [16] his elephants, horses, treasures, and Roman deserters, they demanded that he surrender himself—an act which is the worst possible misfortune for a prince and can never constitute a condition of peace.

Finally, they judged kings for their personal faults and crimes. They heard the complaints of all those who had some dispute with Philip; they sent deputies to provide for their safety. And they had Perseus accused before them for some murders and quarrels with citizens of allied cities.

Since a general's glory was judged by the amount of gold and silver carried at his triumph, he left nothing to the conquered enemy. Rome continually grew richer, and every war put it in a position to undertake another.

The peoples who were friends or allies all ruined themselves by the immense presents they gave to keep or gain favor, and half the money sent to the Romans for this purpose would have been enough to conquer them.[17]

Masters of the world, they assigned all its treasures to themselves, and in plundering were less unjust as conquerors than as legislators. Learning that Ptolemy, king of Cyprus, had immense riches, on the motion of a tribune they enacted [18] a law by which they gave themselves the estate of a living man and a fortune confiscated from an allied prince.

Soon the cupidity of individuals finished carrying off whatever had escaped public avarice. The magistrates and governors sold their injustices to kings. Two competitors ruined themselves vying with each other to buy a protection that was always doubtful against any rival whose funds were not entirely exhausted. For not even the justice of brigands, who bring a certain honesty to the practice of crime, was to be found among the Romans. In short, since legitimate or usurped rights were sustained by money alone, princes despoiled temples and confiscated the property of the richest citizens in order to get it. A thousand crimes were committed just to give the Romans all the money in the world.

But nothing served Rome better than the respect it commanded everywhere. It immediately reduced kings to silence, and, as it were, stupefied them. Not only was the extent of their power at stake, but their own person came under attack. To risk a war with Rome was to expose oneself to captivity, death and the infamy of the triumph. Thus, kings who lived amid pomp and delights did not dare cast a steady glance at the Roman people. And losing courage, they hoped, through their patience and baseness, to gain some delay of the calamities with which they were menaced.[19]

Please observe the conduct of the Romans. After the defeat of Antiochus, they were masters of Africa, Asia, and Greece with scarcely any cities of their own there. It seemed that they conquered only to give. But so thoroughly did they remain the masters that when they made war on some prince, they overwhelmed him, so to speak, with the weight of the whole world.

The time had not yet come to take over the conquered countries. If they had kept the cities captured from Philip, they would have opened the eyes of the Greeks. If, after the Second Punic War or the war with Antiochus, they had taken lands in Africa or Asia, they would have been unable to preserve conquests established on so slight a foundation.[20]

It was necessary to wait until all nations were accustomed to obeying as free states and allies before commanding them as subjects, and until they disappeared little by little into the Roman republic.

Look at the treaty they made with the Latins after the victory of Lake Regillus.[21] It was one of the main foundations of their power. Not a single word is found there that might arouse suspicions of empire.

It was a slow way of conquering. They vanquished a people and were content to weaken it. They imposed conditions on it which undermined it insensibly. If it revolted, it was reduced still further, and it became a subject people without anyone being able to say when its subjection began.

Thus Rome was really neither a monarchy nor a republic, but the head of a body formed by all the peoples of the world.

If the Spaniards had followed this system after the conquest of Mexico and Peru, they would not have been forced to destroy everything in order to preserve everything.

It is the folly of conquerors to want to give their laws and customs to all peoples. This serves no purpose, for people are capable of obeying in any form of government.

But since Rome imposed no general laws, the various peoples had no dangerous ties among themselves. They constituted a body only by virtue of a common obedience, and, without being compatriots, they were all Romans.

The objection will perhaps be made that empires founded on the laws of fiefs [e] have never been either durable or powerful. But no two systems in the world were so antithetical as the Roman and the barbarian. In a word, the former was the work of strength, the latter of weakness; in one, subjection was extreme, in the other, independence. In the countries conquered by the Germanic nations, power was in the hands of the vassals and only legal authority in the hands of the prince. The exact opposite was true with the Romans.

NOTES

1. One example of this is the war against the Dalmatians. See Polybius (XXXII, 19).
2. See especially their treaty with the Jews, in the first book of the *Maccabees, 8.*
3. Ariarathes made a sacrifice to the gods, Polybius tells us (XXXIV, 15), to thank them for his having obtained this alliance.
4. See Polybius on the cities of Greece.
5. Son of Philopator.
6. This was the case with Antiochus.
7. The prohibition made even before the war against Antiochus' crossing into Europe was extended against the other kings.
8. Appian, *The War with Mithridates* (13).
9. A fragment of Dionysius, taken from *The Extract of Embassies.*
10. Livy, VII (XLV, 29).
11. As happened to Ariarathes and Holophernes, in Cappadocia. Appian, *The Syrian Wars* (XLVII).
12. In order to be able to ruin Syria through their regency, they declared themselves for the son of Antiochus, who was still an infant, and against Demetrius, who was their hostage

---

[e] "Laws of fiefs" refers to the political structure of feudalism.

and who begged them to give him his due, saying that Rome was his mother and the senators his fathers.

13. It was an invariable practice, as we can see from history.
14. See how they conducted themselves in the Macedonian war.
15. They acted the same way with the Samnites, the Lusitanians, and the peoples of Corsica. On these last-named, see a fragment of Dio, I.
16. They acted the same way with Viriathus. After getting him to return their deserters, they demanded that he surrender his arms, to which neither he nor his men could consent. Fragment of Dio.
17. The presents the senate sent the kings were mere bagatelles, like a chair and a baton of ivory, or some magisterial robe.
18. Florus, III, 9.
19. They hid their power and riches from the Romans as much as they could. On this point, see a fragment of Dio. I.
20. They did not dare expose their own colonies there. They preferred to plant an everlasting jealousy between the Carthaginians and Masinissa, and to use the help of the one and the other to subdue Macedonia and Greece.
21. Dionysius of Halicarnassus reports it, VI, 95, Oxford edition.

CHAPTER VII

HOW MITHRIDATES WAS ABLE

TO RESIST THEM

Of all the kings the Romans attacked, only Mithridates defended himself with courage and posed a threat to them.

His states were ideally located for waging war against them. They bordered on the inaccessible country of the Caucasus—filled with fierce nations that could be drawn upon—and from there extended to the Black Sea. Mithridates covered this sea with his vessels and continually made trips to buy new armies of Scythians. Asia was open to his invasions. He was rich, because his cities on the Black Sea carried on an advantageous commerce with nations less industrious than themselves.

Proscriptions, the practice of which began in those times, forced many Romans to leave their country. Mithridates welcomed them with open arms. He formed legions in which he enrolled them and which were his best troops.[1]

On its side, Rome, suffering from civil dissensions, occupied with more pressing evils, neglected Asian affairs and let Mithridates pursue his victories or rest after his defeats.

Nothing had been more ruinous to most of the kings than their manifest desire for peace. This deterred all other peoples from sharing with them a peril from which they themselves wanted so much to escape. But Mithridates immediately let it be known to all that he was an enemy of the Romans and always would be.

Finally, the cities of Greece and Asia, feeling the yoke of the Romans weigh more heavily on them every day, placed their confidence in this barbarian king who summoned them to liberty.

This state of affairs led to three great wars which form one of the finest portions of Roman history. For here we do not see princes already vanquished by indulgences and pride, like Antiochus and Tigranes, or by fear, like Philip, Perseus, and Jugurtha, but a magnanimous king, who, in his adversities, like a lion viewing his wounds, was only made more indignant by them.

These wars were peculiar because of their continual and always unexpected revolutions. For if Mithridates could easily replenish his armies, it was also the case that in reverses, when obedience and discipline were needed most, his barbarian troops abandoned him. If he had the art of inciting peoples and making cities revolt, he in turn experienced perfidies on the part of his captains, his children, and his wives. Finally, if he had unskilful Roman generals to deal with, at various times Sulla, Lucullus, and Pompey were also sent against him.

This prince defeated the Roman generals and conquered Asia, Macedonia, and Greece. Vanquished in turn by Sulla, reduced, by treaty, to his old borders, harassed by Roman generals, he again became their victor and the conqueror of Asia. Then, pursued by Lucullus and followed into his own country, he was forced to withdraw to Tigranes' realm, and seeing him hopelessly lost after defeat, and now relying only on himself, he took refuge in his own states and reestablished himself there.

Pompey succeeded Lucullus, and Mithridates was overwhelmed by him. He fled from his states, and, crossing the

Araxes, marched from one danger to another through the country of the Lazians.ᵃ Collecting on his way whatever barbarians he found, he appeared at the Bosporus to confront his son Machares, who had made peace with the Romans.[2]

In the abyss in which he found himself, he devised a scheme for carrying the war to Italy and going to Rome with the same nations that subdued it some centuries later, and by the same route.[3]

Betrayed by Pharnaces, another of his sons, and by an army dismayed at the magnitude of his enterprises and of the dangers he was about to seek, he died a king.

It was then that Pompey, in a rapid succession of victories, completed the splendid work of Rome's greatness. He joined an infinite number of countries to the body of its empire—which served the show of Roman magnificence more than its true power. And although it seemed, from placards carried in his triumph, that he had increased the public revenues by more than a third, power was not increased, and public liberty was only the more endangered.[4]

NOTES

1. Frontinus, *Stratagems,* II (3), says that Archelaus, Mithridates' lieutenant, fighting against Sulla, placed his scythe-bearing chariots in the first ranks, his phalanx in the second, and his auxiliaries, armed in Roman style, in the third, *mixtis fugitivis Italiae, quorum pervicaciae multum fidebat* (with an admixture of Italian fugitive slaves in whose doggedness he had much confidence). Mithridates even made

---

ᵃ Araxes: a river in Asia Minor, flowing eastward into the Caspian Sea: Lazians: a people living at the eastern end of the Black Sea.

an alliance with Sertorius. Also see Plutarch, *Life of Lucul-lus* (7).

2. Mithridates had made him king of the Bosporus. At the news of his father's arrival, he killed himself.
3. See Appian, *The War with Mithridates* (XVI, 109).
4. See Plutarch, in the *Life of Pompey* (39), and Zonaras, II (X, 5).

CHAPTER VIII

THE DISSENSIONS THAT ALWAYS

EXISTED IN THE CITY

While Rome conquered the world, a secret war was going on within its walls. Its fires were like those of volcanoes which burst forth whenever some matter comes along to increase their activity.

After the expulsion of the kings, the government had become aristocratic. The patrician families alone [1] obtained all the magistracies, all the dignities, and consequently all military and civil honors. [2]

To prevent the return of the kings, the patricians sought to intensify the feelings existing in the minds of the people. But they did more than they intended: by imbuing the people with hatred for kings, they gave them an immoderate desire for liberty. Since royal authority had passed entirely into the hands of the consuls, the people felt they lacked the liberty they were being asked to love. They therefore sought to reduce the consulate, to get plebeian magistrates, and to share the curule magistracies [a] with the nobles. The patricians were forced to grant everything they demanded, for in a city where poverty was public virtue, and where riches—the secret road

[a] Curule magistracies: those conferring the right of using the *sella curulis* or chair of state—namely, those of the dictator, consuls, praetors, censors, and curule aediles.

to the acquisition of power—were scorned, birth and dignities could not confer great advantages. Thus, power had to return to the greatest number, and gradually the aristocracy had to change into a popular state.

Those who obey a king are less tormented by envy and jealousy than those who live under an hereditary aristocracy. The prince is so distant from his subjects that he is almost unseen by them. And he is so far above them that they can conceive of no relationship on his part capable of shocking them. But the nobles who govern are visible to all, and are not so elevated that odious comparisons are not constantly made. Therefore it has at all times been seen, and is still seen, that the people detest senators. Those republics where birth confers no part in the government are in this respect the most fortunate, for the people are less likely to envy an authority they give to whomever they wish and take back whenever they fancy.

Discontented with the patricians, the people withdrew to Mons Sacer.[b] Deputies were sent to appease them, and since they all promised to help each other in case the patricians did not keep their pledge[3]—which would have caused constant seditions and disturbed all the operations of the magistrates— it was judged better to create a magistracy that could prevent injustices from being done to plebeians.[4] But, due to a malady eternal in man, the plebeians, who had obtained tribunes to defend themselves, used them for attacking. Little by little they removed the prerogatives of the patricians—which produced continual contention. The people were supported, or rather, animated by their tribunes; and the patricians were defended by the senate, which was almost completely composed of them, was more inclined to the old maxims, and

---

[b] Mons Sacer: a low range of hills about three miles from Rome, consecrated by the people to Jupiter after their secession.

was fearful that the populace would elevate some tribune
to tyranny.

In their own behalf the people employed their strength and
their voting superiority, their refusal to go to war, their
threats to withdraw, the partiality of their laws, and, finally,
their judgments against those who resisted them too staunchly.
The senate defended itself by means of its wisdom, its justice,
and the love of country it inspired; by its benefactions and
a wise use of the republic's treasury; by the respect the people
had for the glory of the leading families and the virtue of
illustrious men; [5] by religion itself, the old institutions, and
the skipping of assembly days on the pretext that the auspices
had not been favorable; by clients; by the opposition of one
tribune to another; by the creation of a dictator, [6] the occupations of a new war, or misfortunes which united all interests; finally, by a paternal condescension in granting the
people a part of their demands in order to make them abandon
the rest, and by the constant maxim of preferring the preservation of the republic to the prerogatives of any order or of any
magistracy whatsoever.

With the passage of time, the plebeians had so reduced
the patricians that this distinction [7] among families became
empty and all were elevated to honors indifferently. Then
there arose new disputes between the common people, agitated by their tribunes, and the leading families, whether
patrician or plebeian, who were called nobles and who had
on their side the senate, which was composed of them. But
since the old morals no longer existed, since individuals had
immense riches, and since riches necessarily confer power,
the nobles resisted with more force than had the patricians,
and this was the cause of the death of the Gracchi and of
several who worked for their scheme. [8]

I must mention a magistracy that greatly contributed to
upholding Rome's government—that of the censors. They

took the census of the people, and, what is more, since the strength of the republic consisted in discipline, austerity of morals, and the constant observance of certain customs, they corrected the abuses that the law had not foreseen, or that the ordinary magistrate could not punish.[9] There are bad examples which are worse than crimes, and more states have perished by the violation of their moral customs than by the violation of their laws. In Rome, everything that could introduce dangerous novelties, change the heart or mind of the citizen, and deprive the state—if I dare use the term—of perpetuity, all disorders, domestic or public, were reformed by the censors. They could evict from the senate whomever they wished, strip a knight of the horse the public maintained for him, and put a citizen in another tribe and even among those who supported the burdens of the city without participating in its privileges.[10]

M. Livius stigmatized the people itself, and, of the thirty-five tribes, he placed thirty-four in the ranks of those who had no part in the privileges of the city.[11] "For," he said, "after condemning me you made me consul and censor. You must therefore have betrayed your trust either once, by inflicting a penalty on me, or twice, by making me consul and then censor."

M. Duronius, a tribune of the people, was driven from the senate by the censors because, during his magistracy, he had abrogated the law limiting expenses at banquets.[12]

The censorship was a very wise institution. The censors could not take a magistracy from anyone, because that would have disturbed the exercise of public power,[13] but they imposed the loss of order and rank, and deprived a citizen, so to speak, of his personal worth.

Servius Tullius had created the famous division by centuries, as Livy [14] and Dionysius of Halicarnassus [15] have so well explained to us. He had distributed one hundred and ninety-three centuries into six classes, and put the whole of the common people into the last century, which alone formed the sixth class. One sees that this disposition excluded the common people from the suffrage, not by right but in fact. Later it was ruled that the division by tribes would be followed in voting, except in certain cases. There were thirty-five tribes, each with a voice—four in the city and thirty-one in the countryside. The leading citizens, all farmers, naturally entered the tribes of the countryside. Those of the city received the common people,[16] which, enclosed there, had very little influence on affairs, and this was regarded as the salvation of the republic. And when Fabius relocated among the four city tribes the lower classes whom Appius Claudius had spread among all the tribes, he acquired the surname of Very Great.[17;c] Every five years the censors took a look at the actual situation of the republic, and distributed the people among the different tribes in such a manner that the tribunes and the ambitious could not gain control of the voting, and the people themselves could not abuse their power.

The government of Rome was admirable. From its birth, abuses of power could always be corrected by its constitution, whether by means of the spirit of the people, the strength of the senate, or the authority of certain magistrates.

Carthage perished because it could not even endure the hand of its own Hannibal when abuses had to be cut away. Athens fell because its errors seemed so sweet to it that it did not wish to recover from them. And, among us, the republics of Italy, which boast of the perpetuity of their government, ought only to boast of the perpetuity of their abuses. Thus, they have no more liberty than Rome had in the time of the decemvirs.[18]

The government of England is wiser, because a body [d]

---

[c] In Latin, *Maximus.*

[d] For Montesquieu's analysis of the English Parliament, see *The Spirit of the Laws,* XI, 6.

there continually examines it and continually examines itself. And such are its errors that they never last long and are often useful for the spirit of watchfulness they give the nation.

In a word, a free government—that is, a government constantly subject to agitation—cannot last if it is not capable of being corrected by its own laws.

NOTES

1. The patricians even had something of a sacred quality: they alone could take the auspices. See Appius Claudius' harangue in Livy, VI (40, 41).

2. For example, they alone could have a triumph, since only they could be consuls and command the armies.

3. Zonaras, II (VII, 15).

4. Origin of the tribunes of the people.

5. Loving glory and composed of men who had spent their lives at war, the people could not refuse their votes to a great man under whom they had fought. They obtained the right to elect plebeians, and elected patricians. They were forced to tie their own hands in establishing the rule that there would always be one plebeian consul. Thus, the plebeian families which first held office were then continually returned to it, and when the people elevated to honors some nobody like Varro or Marius, it was a kind of victory they won over themselves.

6. To defend themselves, the patricians were in the habit of creating a dictator—which succeeded admirably well for them. But once the plebeians had obtained the power of being elected consuls, they could also be elected dictators —which disconcerted the patricians. See in Livy, VIII (12), how Publius Philo reduced them during his dictatorship; he made three laws which were very prejudicial to them.

7. The patricians retained only some sacerdotal offices and the right to create a magistrate called *interrex*.

8. Like Saturninus and Glaucia.

9. We can see how they degraded those who had favored abandoning Italy after the battle of Cannae, those who had surrendered to Hannibal, and those who—by a mischievous interpretation—had broken their word to him. (Livy, XXIV, 18).

10. This was called: *Aerarium aliquem facere, aut in Caeritum tabulas referre* (to make someone a citizen of the lowest class, or to place him on the list of the [voteless] inhabitants of Caere). He was expelled from his century and no longer had the right to vote.

11. Livy, XXIX (37).

12. Valerius Maximus, II (9).

13. The dignity of senator was not a magistracy.

14. I (42, 43).

15. IV, art. 15 ff.

16. Called *turba forensis* (the rabble of the forum).

17. See Livy, IX (46).

18. Nor even more power.

CHAPTER IX

TWO CAUSES OF ROME'S RUIN

When the domination of Rome was limited to Italy, the republic could easily maintain itself. A soldier was equally a citizen. Every consul raised an army, and other citizens went to war in their turn under his successor. Since the number of troops was not excessive, care was taken to admit into the militia only people who had enough property to have an interest in preserving the city.[1] Finally, the senate was able to observe the conduct of the generals and removed any thought they might have of violating their duty.

But when the legions crossed the Alps and the sea, the warriors, who had to be left in the countries they were subjugating for the duration of several campaigns, gradually lost their citizen spirit. And the generals, who disposed of armies and kingdoms, sensed their own strength and could obey no longer.

The soldiers then began to recognize no one but their general, to base all their hopes on him, and to feel more remote from the city. They were no longer the soldiers of the republic but those of Sulla, Marius, Pompey, and Caesar. Rome could no longer know if the man at the head of an army in a province was its general or its enemy.

As long as the people of Rome were corrupted only by their tribunes, to whom they could grant only their own power, the senate could easily defend itself because it acted with constancy, whereas the populace always went from extreme ardor to extreme weakness. But, when the people could give their favorites a formidable authority abroad, all the wisdom of the senate became useless, and the republic was lost.

What makes free states last a shorter time than others is that both the misfortunes and the successes they encounter almost always cause them to lose their freedom. In a state where the people are held in subjection, however, successes and misfortunes alike confirm their servitude. A wise republic should hazard nothing that exposes it to either good or bad fortune. The only good to which it should aspire is the perpetuation of its condition.

If the greatness of the empire ruined the republic, the greatness of the city ruined it no less.

Rome had subjugated the whole world with the help of the peoples of Italy, to whom it had at different times given various privileges.[2][a] At first most of these peoples did not care very much about the right of Roman citizenship, and some preferred to keep their customs.[3] But when this right meant universal sovereignty, and a man was nothing in the world if he was not a Roman citizen and everything if he was, the peoples of Italy resolved to perish or become Romans. Unable to succeed by their intrigues and entreaties, they took the path of arms. They revolted all along the coast of the Ionian sea; the other allies started to follow them.[4] Forced to fight against those who were, so to speak, the hands with which it enslaved the world, Rome was lost. It was going to be reduced to its walls; it therefore accorded the coveted right of citizenship to the allies who had not yet ceased being loyal,[5] and gradually to all.

After this, Rome was no longer a city whose people had but a single spirit, a single love of liberty, a single hatred

---

[a] In extent and importance, Latin rights were between Roman and Italian rights.

of tyranny—a city where the jealousy of the senate's power
and the prerogatives of the great, always mixed with respect,
was only a love of equality. Once the peoples of Italy became
its citizens, each city brought to Rome its genius, its particular interests, and its dependence on some great protector.[6]
The distracted city no longer formed a complete whole. And
since citizens were such only by a kind of fiction, since they
no longer had the same magistrates, the same walls, the same
gods, the same temples, and the same graves, they no longer
saw Rome with the same eyes, no longer had the same love
of country, and Roman sentiments were no more.

The ambitious brought entire cities and nations to Rome
to disturb the voting or get themselves elected. The assemblies
were veritable conspiracies; a band of seditious men was
called a *comitia.*[b] The people's authority, their laws and even
the people themselves became chimerical things, and the
anarchy was such that it was no longer possible to know
whether the people had or had not adopted an ordinance.[7]

We hear in the authors only of the dissensions that ruined
Rome, without seeing that these dissensions were necessary
to it, that they had always been there and always had to
be. It was the greatness of the republic that caused all the
trouble and changed popular tumults into civil wars. There
had to be dissensions in Rome, for warriors who were so
proud, so audacious, so terrible abroad could not be very
moderate at home. To ask for men in a free state who are
bold in war and timid in peace is to wish the impossible.
And, as a general rule, whenever we see everyone tranquil
in a state that calls itself a republic, we can be sure that
liberty does not exist there.

What is called union in a body politic is a very equivocal
thing. The true kind is a union of harmony, whereby all the

---

[b] These were the assemblies into which the Roman people were
organized for electoral purposes.

parts, however opposed they may appear, cooperate for the general good of society—as dissonances in music cooperate in producing overall concord. In a state where we seem to see nothing but commotion there can be union—that is, a harmony resulting in happiness, which alone is true peace. It is as with the parts of the universe, eternally linked together by the action of some and the reaction of others.

But, in the concord of Asiatic despotism—that is, of all government which is not moderate—there is always real dissension. The worker, the soldier, the lawyer, the magistrate, the noble are joined only inasmuch as some oppress the others without resistance. And, if we see any union there, it is not citizens who are united but dead bodies buried one next to the other.

It is true that the laws of Rome became powerless to govern the republic. But it is a matter of common observation that good laws, which have made a small republic grow large, become a burden to it when it is enlarged. For they were such that their natural effect was to create a great people, not to govern it.

There is a considerable difference between good laws and expedient laws—between those that enable a people to make itself master of others, and those that maintain its power once it is acquired.

There exists in the world at this moment a republic that hardly anyone knows about,[8] and that—in secrecy and silence —increases its strength every day. Certainly, if it ever attains the greatness for which its wisdom destines it, it will necessarily change its laws. And this will not be the work of a legislator but of corruption itself.

Rome was made for expansion, and its laws were admirable for this purpose. Thus, whatever its government had been—whether the power of kings, aristocracy, or a popular state—it never ceased undertaking enterprises that made demands on its conduct, and succeeded in them. It did not prove wiser than all the other states on earth for a day, but continually. It sustained meager, moderate and great prosperity with the same superiority, and had neither successes from which it did not profit, nor misfortunes of which it made no use.

It lost its liberty because it completed the work it wrought too soon.

NOTES

1. The freedmen, and those called *capite censi* (because they had very little property and were only taxed by head) at first were not enrolled in the army except in pressing cases. Servius Tullius had put them into the sixth class, and soldiers were only taken from the first five. But Marius, setting out against Jugurtha, enrolled everyone indifferently: *Milites scribere non more majorum neque, ex classibus, sed uti cujusque libido erat, capite censos plerosque* (He himself, in the meantime, proceeded to enlist soldiers not in the old way, or from the classes, but taking all who were willing to join him, and most of them from the *capite censi*). Sallust, *The Jugurthine War*, LXXXVI. Notice that in the division by tribes, those in the four tribes of the city were almost the same as those who were in the sixth class in the division by centuries.

2. Latin rights, Italian rights.

3. The Aequians said in their assemblies: "Those able to choose have preferred their own laws to the law of the city of Rome, which has been a necessary penalty for those who could not defend themselves against it." Livy, IX (45).

4. The Asculans, Marsians, Vestinians, Marrucinians, Ferentinians, Hirpinians, Pompeianians, Venusinians, Iapygians, Lucanians, Samnites and others. Appian, *The Civil War*, I (39).

5. The Tuscans, Umbrians, and Latins. This led some peoples to submit; and, since they too were made citizens, still others

laid down their arms; and finally there remained only the Samnites, who were exterminated.

6. Just imagine this monstrous head of the peoples of Italy which, by the suffrage of every man, directed the rest of the world.

7. See the *Letters of Cicero to Atticus,* IV, letter 18.

8. The canton of Bern.

CHAPTER X

THE CORRUPTION OF THE

ROMANS

I believe the sect of Epicurus,[a] which was introduced at Rome toward the end of the republic, contributed much toward tainting the heart and mind of the Romans.[1] The Greeks had been infatuated with this sect earlier and thus were corrupted sooner. Polybius tells us that in his time a Greek's oaths inspired no confidence, whereas a Roman was, so to speak, enchained by his.[2]

A fact mentioned in the letters of Cicero to Atticus[3] shows us the extent to which the Romans had changed in this regard since the time of Polybius.

"Memmius," he says, "has just communicated to the senate the agreement his competitor and he had made with the consuls, by which the latter had pledged to favor them in their quest for the next year's consulate. And they, on their part, promised to pay the consuls four hundred thousand

---

[a] Epicurus was a Greek philosopher (341-270 B.C.) who elaborated the doctrine of hedonism in ethics as the proper complement of atheistic atomism in physics. The greatest Roman author in this tradition was Lucretius (99-55 B.C.).

sisterces if they furnished three auguries which would declare that they were present when the people had made the law *curiate*,[4] although they had not been, and two ex-consuls who would affirm that they had assisted in signing the *senatus consultum* which regulated the condition of their provinces, although they had not." How many dishonest men in a single contract!

Aside from the fact that religion is always the best guarantee one can have of the morals of men, it was a special trait of the Romans that they mingled some religious sentiment with their love of country. This city, founded under the best auspices; this Romulus, their king and their god; this Capitol, eternal like the city, and this city, eternal like its founder—these, in earlier times, had made an impression on the mind of the Romans which it would have been desirable to preserve.

The greatness of the state caused the greatness of personal fortunes. But since opulence consists in morals, not riches, the riches of the Romans, which continued to have limits, produced a luxury and profusion which did not.[5] Those who had at first been corrupted by their riches were later corrupted by their poverty. With possessions beyond the needs of private life it was difficult to be a good citizen; with the desires and regrets of one whose great fortune has been ruined, one was ready for every desperate attempt. And, as Sallust says,[6] a generation of men arose who could neither have a patrimony nor endure others having any.

Yet, whatever the corruption of Rome, not every misfortune was introduced there. For the strength of its institutions had been such that it preserved its heroic valor and all of its application to war in the midst of riches, indolence and sensual pleasures—which, I believe, has happened to no other nation in the world.

Roman citizens regarded commerce [7] and the arts as the

occupations of slaves: [8] they did not practice them. If there were any exceptions, it was only on the part of some freedmen who continued their original work. But, in general, the Romans knew only the art of war, which was the sole path to magistracies and honors.[9] Thus, the martial virtues remained after all the others were lost.

NOTES

1. When Cineas discoursed of it at Pyrrhus' table, Fabricius wished that Rome's enemies might all adopt the principles of such a sect. Plutarch, *Life of Pyrrhus* (20).
2. "If you lend a Greek a talent and bind him by ten promises, ten sureties, and as many witnesses, it is impossible for him to keep his word. But among the Romans, whether in accounting for public or private funds, people are trustworthy because of the oath they have taken. The fear of hell has therefore been wisely established, and it is fought today without reason." Polybius, VI (56).
3. IV, letter 18.
4. The law *curiate* conferred military power; and the *senatus consultum* regulated the troops, money and officers that the governor was to have. Now for all that to be done at their fancy, the consuls wanted to fabricate a spurious law and a spurious senatus consultum.
5. The house Cornelia had bought for seventy-five thousand drachmas was bought by Lucullus shortly afterwards for two million five hundred thousand. Plutarch, *Life of Marius* (18).
6. *Ut merito dicatur genitos esse, qui nec ipsi habere possent res familiares, nec alios pati* (So that it was rightly said of Rome that she begot men who could neither keep property themselves nor suffer others to do so). Fragment of Sallust's history, taken from St. Augustine's *The City of God*, II, 18.
7. Romulus permitted free men only two kinds of occupation —agriculture and war. Merchants, artisans, those who paid

rent for their house, and tavern-keepers were not numbered among the citizens. Dionysius of Halicarnassus, II (28), IX (25).

8. Cicero gives the reasons for this in his *Offices,* I, 42.

9. It was necessary to have served ten years, between the ages of sixteen and forty-seven. See Polybius, VI (19).

CHAPTER XI

1. SULLA

2. POMPEY AND CAESAR

I beg permission to avert my eyes from the horrors of the wars of Marius and Sulla. Their appalling history is found in Appian. Over and above the jealousy, ambition, and cruelty of the two leaders, every Roman was filled with frenzy. New citizens and old no longer regarded each other as members of the same republic,[1] and they fought a war which—due to its peculiar character—was civil and foreign at the same time.

Sulla enacted laws well-designed to remove the cause of the existing disorders. They increased the authority of the senate, tempered the power of the people, and regulated that of the tribunes. The whim that made him give up the dictatorship seemed to restore life to the republic. But, in the frenzy of his successes, he had done things that made it impossible for Rome to preserve its liberty.

In his Asian expedition he ruined all military discipline. He accustomed his army to rapine,[2] and gave it needs it never had before. He corrupted for the first time the soldiers who were later to corrupt their captains.

He entered Rome arms in hand, and taught Roman generals to violate the asylum of liberty.[3]

He gave the lands of citizens to the soldiers,[4] and made them forever greedy; from this moment onward, every warrior awaited an occasion that could place in his hands the property of his fellow citizens.

He invented proscriptions, and put a price on the heads of those who were not of his party. After that, it was impossible to adhere to the republic, for with two ambitious men disputing for victory, those who were neutral and partisans only of liberty were sure to be proscribed by whoever won. It was therefore prudent to be an adherent of one or the other.

After him, Cicero tells us,[5] came a man[a] who, in an impious cause, and after a still more shameful victory, not only confiscated the property of individuals but enveloped whole provinces in the same calamity.

In laying down the dictatorship, Sulla had appeared to want only to live under the protection of his own laws. But this action, indicating so much moderation, was itself a consequence of his acts of violence. He had set up forty-seven legions in different places in Italy. "Regarding their fortunes as attached to his life," says Appian, "these men watched over his safety and were always ready to aid or avenge him." [6]

Since the republic necessarily had to perish, it was only a question of how, and by whom, it was to be overthrown.

Two men of equal ambition—except that one did not know how to gain his end as directly as the other—overshadowed all other citizens by their repute, their exploits and their virtues. Pompey was first to appear; Caesar came right after him.

To attract favor to himself, Pompey set aside the laws of Sulla limiting the power of the people. When he had sacrificed the most salutary laws of his country to his ambition,

---

[a] A man: Caesar.

he obtained all he wanted, and the temerity of the people in his behalf knew no bounds.

The laws of Rome had wisely divided public power among a large number of magistracies, which supported, checked and tempered each other. Since they all had only limited power, every citizen was qualified for them, and the people—seeing many persons pass before them one after the other—did not grow accustomed to any in particular. But in these times the system of the republic changed. Through the people the most powerful men gave themselves extraordinary commissions—which destroyed the authority of the people and magistrates, and placed all great matters in the hands of one man, or a few.[7]

Was it necessary to make war on Sertorius? The commission was given to Pompey. On Mithridates? Everyone cried Pompey. Did grain have to be brought to Rome? The people thought themselves lost if Pompey was not appointed. Were the pirates to be destroyed? Only Pompey could do it. And, when Caesar threatened invasion, the senate cried out in its turn and placed its hopes in none but Pompey.

"I really believe," said Marcus [8] to the people "that Pompey—whom the nobles await—will prefer to secure your liberty rather than their domination. But there was a time when each of you had the protection of many, and not all the protection of one, and when it was unheard of that one mortal could give or take away such things."

Since Rome was made for expansion, honors and power had to be united in the same persons, which in times of trouble could fix the admiration of the people on a single citizen.

When one accords honors, one knows precisely what one gives; but when power is joined to them, one cannot say how far it may be stretched.

Excessive preference given to a citizen in a republic always has necessary effects. It either makes the people envious or increases their love beyond measure.

On two occasions Pompey returned to Rome with the power to crush it, but had the moderation to discharge his armies before entering the city and to appear as a simple citizen. These actions, which covered him with glory, had the effect thereafter of causing the senate always to declare itself for him, whatever he did to the prejudice of the laws.

Pompey had a slower and milder ambition than Caesar. The latter wanted to ascend to sovereign power arms in hand, like Sulla. This way of oppressing did not please Pompey. He aspired to the dictatorship, but through the votes of the people. He could not consent to usurp power, but he would have wanted it placed in his hands.

Since the favor of the people is never constant, there were times when Pompey saw his prestige diminish.[9] And he was really upset when men he scorned increased their prestige and used it against him.

This made him do three equally fatal things. He corrupted the people with money, and in elections put a price on the vote of every citizen.

In addition, he used the vilest mobs to disturb the magistrates in their functions, hoping that sober men, tired of living in anarchy, would make him dictator out of despair.

Finally, he joined forces with Caesar and Crassus. Cato said it was their union, not their enmity, that destroyed the republic. Indeed, Rome was in the unfortunate position of being less burdened by civil wars than by peace, which united the views and interests of the leading men and brought nothing but tyranny.

Pompey did not exactly lend his reputation to Caesar, but, without knowing it, he sacrificed it to him. Soon Caesar employed against Pompey the forces Pompey had given him, and even his artifices. He disturbed the city with his emissaries, and gained control over the elections. Consuls, praetors, and tribunes were bought at the price they themselves set.

The senate, which clearly saw Caesar's designs, had recourse to Pompey. It begged him to undertake the defense of the republic—if this name could be used for a government which implored protection from one of its citizens.

I believe that Pompey was ruined more than anything else by his shame at thinking that he had lacked foresight in elevating Caesar as he did. He yielded as slowly as possible to this idea. He did not prepare his defense so that he would not have to admit he had placed himself in jeopardy. He maintained before the senate that Caesar did not dare make war, and because he said it so often, he always repeated it.

One circumstance seems to have given Caesar the opportunity to undertake anything he wanted. Because of an unfortunate conformity of names, the government of Gaul beyond the Alps had been joined to his government of Gaul.

State policy had not permitted armies close to Rome, but neither had it allowed Italy to be entirely emptied of troops. For this reason, considerable forces were kept in Cisalpine Gaul—that is, in the region going from the Rubicon, a small river in Romagna, to the Alps. But to secure the city of Rome against these troops, the famous *senatus consultum* which can still be seen engraved on the road from Rimini to Cesena was issued. It consigned to the infernal gods, and declared guilty of sacrilege and parricide, anyone who passed the Rubicon with a legion, an army or a cohort.

To so important a government another still more considerable was joined—that of Transalpine Gaul, consisting of the regions of southern France. This gave Caesar a chance to wage war for several years on all the peoples he wanted. It made his soldiers grow older with him and enabled him to conquer them no less than the barbarians. If Caesar had not had the government of Transalpine Gaul, he would not have corrupted his soldiers, nor made his name respected by so many victories. If he had not had that of Cisalpine Gaul,

Pompey could have stopped him at the Alpine pass. As it turned out, Pompey had to abandon Italy at the outset of the war, thus losing for his party the prestige which, in civil wars, is power itself.

The same fright that Hannibal awakened in Rome after the battle of Cannae was spread by Caesar when he crossed the Rubicon. Pompey was distraught and, in the early moments of the war, saw no alternative but the one resorted to last in desperate situations. He could only yield and fly; he departed from Rome, leaving the public treasury behind; nowhere could he delay the victor; he abandoned part of his troops, all of Italy, and crossed the sea.

Much is said of Caesar's good fortune. But this extraordinary man had so many great qualities, without a single defect—although he had many vices—that it would have been very difficult for him not to have been victorious, whatever army he commanded, and not to have governed any republic in which he was born.

After defeating Pompey's lieutenants in Spain, Caesar went to Greece seeking Pompey himself. Pompey, in possession of the sea coast and superior forces, was on the verge of seeing Caesar's army perish from misery and famine. But since his supreme weakness was wanting the approval of others, he could not refrain from lending an ear to the vain talk of his men, who railed at him or reproached him endlessly.[10] "He wishes," said one, "to perpetuate himself in command and be the king of kings, like Agamemnon." "I warn you," said another, "that we shall not eat the figs of Tusculum again this year." Some particular successes he had finally turned the head of this senatorial group. Thus, in order to escape censure, Pompey did something posterity will always censure, and sacrificed so many advantages to engage in battle with new troops against an army that had been victorious so often.

When the survivors of Pharsalus had withdrawn to Africa, Scipio, who commanded them, was never willing to follow Cato's advice and protract the war. Made overconfident by certain advantages, he risked all and lost all. And when Brutus and Cassius reestablished this party, the same precipitation lost the republic a third time.[11]

You will notice that during these civil wars, which lasted so long, Rome's external power kept growing steadily. Under Marius, Sulla, Pompey, Caesar, Anthony, and Augustus, Rome constantly became more terrifying and completed the destruction of all the remaining kings.

No state threatens others with conquest like one in the throes of civil war. Everyone—noble, burgher, artisan, farmer—becomes a soldier, and when peace unites the opposing forces, this state has great advantages over those with nothing but citizens. Besides, during civil wars great men are often produced, because in the confusion those with merit come to the fore. Each man finds his own place and rank, whereas at other times each is given his place, and almost always wrongly. And, to go from the example of the Romans to others that are more recent, the French were never more to be feared abroad than after the quarrels of the houses of Burgundy and Orleans, after the commotions of the League, and after the civil wars during the minorities of Louis XIII and Louis XIV. England was never so respected as under Cromwell, after the wars of the Long Parliament. The Germans acquired superiority over the Turks only after the civil wars of Germany. The Spanish, under Philip V, immediately after the civil wars for the succession, showed a strength in Sicily that amazed Europe. And today we see Persia reborn from the ashes of civil war and humbling the Turks.

Finally, the republic was crushed. And we must not blame it on the ambition of certain individuals; we must blame it on man—a being whose greed for power keeps increasing the more he has of it, and who desires all only because he already possesses much.

If Caesar and Pompey had thought like Cato, others would have thought like Caesar and Pompey; and the republic, destined to perish, would have been dragged to the precipice by another hand.

Caesar pardoned everyone, but it seems to me that moderation shown after usurping everything does not deserve great praise.

In spite of what has been said of Caesar's diligence after Pharsalus, Cicero rightly charges him with procrastination. He tells Cassius that they would never have believed Pompey's party would make such a comeback in Spain and Africa, and that, if they could have foreseen Caesar would toy with his Alexandrian war, they would not have made their peace and would have withdrawn to Africa with Scipio and Cato.[12] Thus, a mad love affair made Caesar take on four wars, and, by not foreseeing the last two, he again put into question what had been decided at Pharsalus.

At first Caesar governed under titles of magistracy—for men are hardly moved by anything but names. And just as the peoples of Asia abhorred the names of consul and proconsul, the peoples of Europe detested the name of king—so that, in those days, these names made for the happiness or despair of all the earth. Caesar did not refrain from trying to have the diadem placed on his head, but, seeing the people stop its acclamations, he rejected it. He made still other attempts;[13] and I cannot comprehend how he could believe that because the Romans endured him as a tyrant, they therefore loved tyranny or believed they had done what they had.

One day when the senate was conferring certain honors upon him, he neglected to rise; and it was then that the gravest members of this body lost all remaining patience.

Men are never more offended than when their ceremonies and practices are flouted. Seeking to oppress them is sometimes a proof of the esteem one has for them; flouting their customs is always a mark of contempt.

At all times an enemy of the senate, Caesar could not conceal the scorn he felt for that body, which had become almost ridiculous since its loss of power. For this reason, his clemency itself was insulting. It was observed that he did not pardon but rather disdained to punish.

He carried scorn to the point where he himself decreed *senatus consulta;* he signed them with the names of the first senators who came to mind. "I sometimes learn," says Cicero,[14] "that a *senatus consultum,* passed on my recommendation, has been carried into Syria and Armenia before I knew a thing about it. And several princes have written me letters of thanks for advising that they receive the title of king when I was not only ignorant of their being kings but of their very existence."

From the letters of some great men of this time,[15] attributed to Cicero because most are by him, we can see the dejection and despair of the foremost men of the republic at this sudden revolution depriving them of their honors and even their occupations. When the senate no longer had a function, the respect they had enjoyed everywhere on earth they could only hope to win in the cabinet of one man. And this is much more obvious in these letters than in the treatises of historians. They are the *chef d'oeuvre* of the naiveté of men united by a common affliction, and of an age when false politeness had not spread lying everywhere. In short, we do not see in them men who wish to deceive each other, as in most of our modern letters, but unhappy friends who seek to tell each other everything.

It was quite difficult for Caesar to defend his life. Most of the conspirators were of his own party, or had been heaped with benefits by him.[16] And the reason for this is quite natural: they had found great advantages in his victory, but the more their fortune improved, the more they began to partake of the common misfortune.[17] For to a man who has nothing it makes rather little difference, in certain respects, under what kind of government he lives.

Moreover, there was a certain law of nations [b]—an opinion held in all the republics of Greece and Italy—according to which the assassin of someone who had usurped sovereign power was regarded as a virtuous man. Especially in Rome, after the expulsion of the kings, the law was precise, and its precedents established. The republic put arms in the hand of every citizen, made him a magistrate for the moment, and recognized him as its defender.

Brutus [18] even dares tell his friends that if his own father returned to earth, he would kill him just the same.[c] And although the continuation of the tyranny gradually brought about the disappearance of this spirit of liberty, conspiracies were constantly reviving at the beginning of Augustus' reign.

It was an overpowering love of country which—taking leave of the ordinary rules for crimes and virtues—hearkened

---

[b] The term *law of nations* referred either to primarily unwritten rules of justice regulating the relations among nations (*i.e.,* to international law, as at the beginning of chapter I above) or to laws (written and unwritten) common to all or most nations, as in the present instance. But Montesquieu applies it to a belief about tyrannicide confined to the republics of Greece and Italy of that day. Compare Chapter XV, par. 4, where it is used even more narrowly. See St. Thomas Aquinas, *Summa Theologica,* first part of the second part, Q 95, art. 4; Grotius *Of the Law of War and Peace,* I, 1 (14); Montesquieu, *The Spirit of the Laws,* I, 3.

[c] This sentence makes little obvious sense, because Montesquieu has omitted the part where Brutus says that he would not concede even to his own father (were he to return to earth) the things he would not endure in Caesar. See Cicero's *Letters* edited by Shuckburgh (London, 1909), vol. 4, p. 245.

only to itself and saw neither citizen, friend, benefactor, nor father. Virtue seemed to forget itself in order to surpass itself, and it made men admire as divine an action that at first could not be approved because it was atrocious.

Indeed, was it not impossible to punish the crime of Caesar, who lived under a free government, in any other way than by assassination? And was not asking why he had not been proceeded against by open force or by the laws the same as asking that his crimes be punished?

NOTES

1. So that he himself rather than Sulla would receive the commission for the war against Mithridates, Marius, with the help of the tribune, Sulpicius, had spread the eight new tribes of the peoples of Italy among the old tribes. This gave the Italians control over the voting, and they, for the most part, were in Marius' party, while the senate and the old citizens were in Sulla's.
2. See the portrait of this army given us by Sallust in *The Conspiracy of Catiline* (11, 12).
3. *Fugatis Marii copiis, primus urbem Romam cum armis ingressus est* (The troops of Marius having fled, he was the first to enter the city of Rome with arms). Fragment of John of Antioch, in *The Extract of Virtues and Vices.*
4. In the beginning, part of the lands of the conquered enemy was indeed distributed; but Sulla gave out the lands of citizens.
5. *Offices*, II, 8.
6. We can see what happened after Caesar's death.
7. *Plebis opes imminutae, paucorum potentia crevit* (The power of the people was reduced, and the authority of the few increased). Sallust, *The Conspiracy of Catiline* (39).
8. Fragment of Sallust's *History.*
9. See Plutarch.
10. See Plutarch, *Life of Pompey.*

11. This is well explained in Appian, *The Civil War*, IV (108 ff).
12. *Letters to His Friends*, XV (letter 15).
13. He dismissed the tribunes of the people.
14. *Letters to His Friends*, IX (letter 15).
15. See the letters of Cicero and Servius Sulpicius.
16. Decimus Brutus, Caius Casca, Trebonius, Tullius Cimber, and Minutius Basillus were friends of Caesar. Appian, *The Civil War*, II (113).
17. I do not speak of a tyrant's satellites, who would share his ruin, but of his companions in a free government.
18. *Letters of Brutus*, in the collection of those of Cicero (I, 16).

CHAPTER XII

THE CONDITION OF ROME

AFTER CAESAR'S DEATH

So impossible was it for the republic to be reestablished that something entirely unprecedented happened: the tyrant was no more, but there was no liberty either. For the causes that had destroyed the republic still remained.

The conspirators had only made plans for the conspiracy, not for following it up.

After the deed was done, they withdrew to the Capitol. The senate did not meet, and the next day, Lepidus, who was looking for trouble, seized the Roman forum with armed men.

The veteran soldiers, who feared the immense gifts they had received would not be repeated, entered Rome. This made the senate give approval to all Caesar's acts, and, for the purpose of conciliating the extremes, grant an amnesty to the conspirators—which produced a counterfeit peace.

Before his death, in preparation for his expedition against the Parthians, Caesar had appointed magistrates for several years, so that his own men might maintain the tranquillity of his government while he was gone. Thus, after his death, his partisans enjoyed resources for a long time.

Since the senate had approved all Caesar's acts without

restriction, and since their execution was delegated to the consuls, Antony, who was a consul, seized his ledgers, won over his secretary, and had inscribed in the ledgers whatever he wanted. In this way the dictator reigned more imperiously than during his lifetime, for Antony did what Caesar would never have done. The money he would never have distributed was distributed by Antony, and every man who bore a grudge against the republic suddenly found a reward in Caesar's ledgers.

As a further misfortune, Caesar had amassed immense sums for his expedition and stored them in the temple of Ops. Antony, with his ledger, disposed of them as he wished.

The conspirators had resolved to throw Caesar's body into the Tiber.[1] They would have met with no obstacle, for in the moments of shock which follow an unexpected action, it is easy to do whatever one dares. But it was not done,[a] and this is what happened.

The senate thought itself obliged to permit Caesar's obsequies, and indeed, since it had not declared him a tyrant, it could not refuse him burial. Now it was a Roman custom, highly praised by Polybius,[b] to carry images of their ancestors in funerals and then deliver a funeral oration for the deceased. Antony, as the orator, showed the people Caesar's bloody robe, read them his will, in which he bestowed great bounties upon them, and stirred them to such a pitch that they set fire to the conspirators' houses.

We have an admission from Cicero, who governed the senate during the whole affair,[2] that it would have been better to act with vigor and risk death, and that no one would have died either. But he exculpates himself by claiming that by

---

[a] At this point the Pléiade edition includes a footnote, considered as Montesquieu's own, to Suetonius, *Julius,* 82.

[b] See Polybius, VI, 53.

the time the senate was assembled, it was too late. And anyone who knows the importance of a moment in affairs in which the people have so large a part will not be surprised at this.

And another accident was involved. While games were in progress honoring Caesar, a comet with a long tail appeared for seven days. The people believed his soul had been admitted into heaven.

It was indeed customary among the peoples of Greece and Asia to build temples to the kings and even the proconsuls who had governed them.[3] They were permitted to do these things as the strongest evidence they could give of their servitude. Even the Romans could accord divine honors to their ancestors in their lararia or private temples.[c] But I do not see that any Roman, from Romulus to Caesar, had been numbered among the public divinities.[4]

The government of Macedonia had fallen to Antony; he wanted that of the Gauls instead, and it is easy to see why. Decimus Brutus had Cisalpine Gaul and Antony wanted to drive him out because he refused to turn it over to him. This produced a civil war, in which the senate declared Antony an enemy of his country.

Cicero had made the mistake of working to elevate Octavius in order to ruin Anthony, his personal enemy. And instead of trying to make the people forget Caesar, he had put Caesar back before their eyes.

Octavius conducted himself adroitly with Cicero. He flattered him, praised him, consulted him, and employed all the artifices of which vanity is never distrustful.

Almost all ventures are spoiled by the fact that those who undertake them usually seek—in addition to the main objec-

---

[c] Lararium: a private chapel in which the lares, or tutelary gods, were placed.

tive—certain small, personal successes which flatter their self-love [d] and give them self-satisfaction.

I believe that if Cato had preserved himself for the republic, he would have given a completely different turn to events. Cicero's talents admirably suited him for a secondary role, but he was not fit for the main one. His genius was superb, but his soul was often common. With Cicero, virtue was the accessory, with Cato, glory.[5] Cicero always thought of himself first, Cato always forgot about himself. The latter wanted to save the republic for its own sake, the former in order to boast of it.

I could continue the comparison by saying that when Cato foresaw, Cicero feared, that where Cato hoped, Cicero was confident, that the former always saw things dispassionately, the latter through a hundred petty passions.

Antony was defeated at Mutina, but the two consuls, Hirtius and Pansa, lost their lives there. The senate, believing it had things under control, considered reducing Octavius, who, for his part, stopped working against Antony, led his army to Rome, and had himself declared consul.

This is how Cicero, who boasted that his robe had destroyed Antony's armies, presented the republic with an enemy even more dangerous because his name was more beloved and his rights, in appearance, more legitimate.[6]

After his defeat, Antony took refuge in Transalpine Gaul, where he was received by Lepidus. These two men united with Octavius, and they traded off to each other the lives of their friends and enemies.[7] Lepidus remained in Rome. The

---

[d] Unlike Rousseau, Montesquieu does not carefully distinguish between *amour-propre* (normally "pride" or "vanity" but, in the context, better translated as "self-love") and *amour de soi* ("love of oneself"). Here, *amour-propre* is used as if it were synonomous with the word *vanité* ("vanity") in the preceding sentence; but in the last paragraph of this chapter it signifies a more general

other two went looking for Brutus and Cassius, and they found them in those places where mastery of the world was contested three times over.

Brutus and Cassius killed themselves with inexcusable precipitation, and we cannot read this chapter in their lives without pitying the republic which was thus abandoned. Cato had killed himself at the end of the tragedy; these began it, in a sense, by their death.

Several reasons can be given for this practice of committing suicide that was so common among the Romans: the advances of the Stoic sect, which encouraged it; the establishment of triumphs and slavery, which made many great men think they must not survive a defeat; the advantage those accused of some crime gained by bringing death upon themselves, rather than submitting to a judgment whereby their memory would be tarnished and their property confiscated; [8] a kind of point of honor, more reasonable, perhaps, than that which today leads us to slaughter our friend for a gesture or word; finally, a great opportunity for heroism, each man putting an end to the part he played in the world wherever he wished.

We could add to these a great facility in executing the deed. When the soul is completely occupied with the action it is about to perform, with the motive determining it, with the peril it is going to avoid, it does not really see death, for passion makes us feel but never see.

Self-love, the love of our own preservation, is transformed in so many ways, and acts by such contrary principles, that it leads us to sacrifice our being for the love of our being. And such is the value we set on ourselves that we consent

---

and fundamental element of man's nature best described as self-love, of which vanity is but one derivative. It is this latter use that Rousseau chose to distinguish by the name *amour de soi,* or "love of oneself." See Rousseau's *First and Second Discourses,* edited by Roger Masters (New York, 1964), pp. 130, 221-2, 236.

to cease living because of a natural and obscure instinct that makes us love ourselves more than our very life.ᵉ

NOTES

1. This would not have been without precedent. After Tiberius Gracchus had been killed, Lucretius, an aedile, who thereafter was called Vespillo, threw his body into the Tiber. Aurelius Victor, *Illustrious Men of Rome* (64).
2. *Letters to Atticus,* XIV, letter 16.
3. See the *Letters of Cicero to Atticus,* V (21), on this point, and the remark of the Abbé de Montgault.
4. Dio says that the triumvirs, who all hoped to take Caesar's place some day, did everything they could to increase the honors accorded him. XLVII (18, 19).
5. *Esse quam videri bonus malebat; itaque quominus gloriam petebat, eo magis illam assequebatur* (He preferred to be rather than to appear virtuous; and thus, the less he sought glory, the more it pursued him). Sallust, *The Conspiracy of Cataline* (54).
6. He was Caesar's heir and his son by adoption.
7. Their cruelty was so irrational that they ordered everyone to rejoice in the proscriptions, on pain of death. See Dio (XLVII, 14).
8. *Eorum qui de se statuebant humabantur corpora, manebant testamenta, pretium festinandi* (Those who passed sentence on themselves were rewarded for their dispatch by being allowed burial and having their wills respected). Tacitus, *Annals,* VI (29).

ᵉ The following passage appeared in the original edition of 1734 but was dropped from the edition of 1748, presumably by Montesquieu himself, only to reappear in the collected works of 1758 recently reprinted by Nagel. It reads: "It is certain that men have become less free, less courageous, less disposed to great enterprises than they were when, by means of this power which one assumed, one could at any moment escape from every other power."

CHAPTER XIII

AUGUSTUS

Sextus Pompey held Sicily and Sardinia. He was master of the sea, and had with him countless fugitives and exiles who were fighting with their last remaining hopes at stake. Octavius waged two quite laborious wars against him, and, after many failures, vanquished him through the skill of Agrippa.

The lives of the conspirators had almost all come to an unhappy end.[1] And it was quite natural that men at the head of a party which was beaten so many times, in wars where no quarter was given, should have died violent deaths. People drew the conclusion, however, that a heavenly vengeance was punishing Caesar's murderers and condemning their cause.

Octavius won over Lepidus' soldiers and stripped him of the power of the triumvirate. He even begrudged him the consolation of leading an obscure life, and forced him to be present, as a private individual, in the popular assemblies.

It is satisfying to see this Lepidus humiliated. He was the most wicked citizen in the republic—always the first to begin disturbances, constantly forming evil projects in which he was forced to associate with cleverer men than himself. A modern author has amused himself by eulogizing him,[2] and cites Antony, who, in one of his letters, calls him a gentleman. But a gentleman for Antony ought hardly to be one for others.

I believe Octavius to be the only one of all the Roman

captains who won his soldiers' affection even while repeatedly
giving them signs of his natural cowardice. In those days the
soldiers valued the liberality of a general more than his courage. Perhaps it was even lucky for him not to have had the
valor that can win dominion, and perhaps this itself helped
him win it, since people feared him less. It is not impossible
that the things which dishonored him most were those that
served him best. If from the first he had displayed a great
soul, everyone would have distrusted him. And if he had
been bold he would not have given Antony the time to engage
in all the extravagances that caused his downfall.

Preparing himself against Octavius, Antony swore to
his soldiers that he would reestablish the republic two months
after his victory. This shows that even the soldiers were
anxious for the liberty of their country, although they continually destroyed it—there being nothing so blind as an army.

The battle of Actium took place; Cleopatra fled, carrying
Antony away with her. It is certain that she betrayed him
afterwards.[3] Perhaps, with a woman's unbelievable spirit of
coquetry, she had formed the design of bringing to her feet
still a third master of the world.

A woman for whom Antony had sacrificed the whole
world betrayed him. So many captains and kings whose power
he had extended or established failed him. And, as if generosity had been linked to servitude, a troop of gladiators
maintained an heroic fidelity to him. Cover a man with
benefits and the first idea you inspire in him is to seek the
means of preserving them; they are so many new interests
you give him to defend.

A surprising feature of these wars is that a single battle
almost always decided the matter, and a single defeat was
irreparable.

Roman soldiers did not really have party spirit. They did
not fight for a certain thing, but for a certain person; they
knew only their leader, who bound them to him by immense

hopes. But since a defeated leader was no longer in a position to fulfill his promises, they turned to someone else. The provinces did not enter into the quarrel with any greater interest because it was of little importance to them whether the senate or the people had the upper hand. Thus, no sooner was one of the leaders defeated than they gave themselves to the other; [4] for each city had to think of justifying itself to the victor, who had immense promises to keep to his soldiers and had to sacrifice to them the most culpable communities.

In France we have had two sorts of civil wars. Some had religion as a pretext, and they endured because their motive continued after victory. The others did not really have any motive, but were instigated by the levity or ambition of some powerful men, and were stifled at once.

Augustus (this is the name flattery gave Octavius) established order—that is, a durable servitude. For in a free state in which sovereignty has just been usurped, whatever can establish the unlimited authority of one man is called good order, and whatever can maintain the honest liberty of the subjects is called commotion, dissension, or bad government.

All the men with ambitious projects had labored to inject a kind of anarchy into the republic. Pompey, Crassus, and Caesar succeeded marvelously at this. They established an impunity for all public crimes; they abolished whatever could stop the corruption of morals or make for effective public order.[a] And as good legislators attempt to make their citizens better, so these labored to make them worse. They therefore introduced the practice of corrupting the people with money; and if someone was accused of intrigues, he also corrupted the judges. They disturbed elections with all kinds of violence; and if someone was brought to justice, he intimidated the judges as well.[5] The very authority of the people was destroyed—witness Gabinius, who after reestablishing Ptol-

---

[a] Public order: *police;* see above, Chapter V, footnote b.

emy [b] by armed might in spite of the people, coldly came to claim a triumph.[6]

These foremost men of the republic sought to make the people weary of their own power and to become necessary by exacerbating the inconveniences of republican government. But once Augustus was master, policy required his working to reestablish order so that everyone would experience the blessings of one-man government.

When Augustus was armed for war, he feared the revolts of soldiers and not the conspiracies of citizens; that is why he treated the soldiers with care and was so cruel to others. When he was at peace, he feared conspiracies; and always having Caesar's destiny before his eyes, he meant to follow a different line of conduct in order to avoid the same fate. This is the key to Augustus' whole life. He wore a breastplate under his robe in the senate; he refused the title of dictator. Whereas Caesar insolently stated that the republic was nothing and that his own word was law, Augustus spoke only of the senate's dignity and of his respect for the republic. His intention, therefore, was to establish that government which was most capable of pleasing without damaging his interests; and he made it aristocratic with respect to civil affairs, and monarchical with respect to military affairs. But since it was not supported by its own strength, this ambiguous government could subsist only so long as it pleased the monarch, and consequently was entirely monarchical.

The question has been asked whether Augustus really had planned to resign his power. But who does not see that if he wanted to it was impossible for him not to succeed? The fact that every ten years he asked to be relieved of his

---

[b] Gabinius had remained governor of Syria even after the senate ordered his return to Rome, and he violated the Roman law against making war outside of his own province when he fought Ptolemy's rebellious subjects in Egypt (*c.* 56 B.C.).

burden and yet kept carrying it proves that he was only act-
ing. These were little artifices for the purpose of being granted
again what he did not think he had sufficiently acquired. I
am being guided by Augustus' whole life; and, although men
are extremely queer, it very rarely happens that they renounce
in a moment what they have sought throughout their life. All
Augustus' actions, all his regulations, tended visibly toward
the establishment of monarchy. Sulla relinquished the dictatorship; but in Sulla's whole life, even in the midst of his acts
of violence, a republican spirit was revealed. All his regulations, although tyrannically executed, always tended toward
a certain form of republic. Sulla, a man of passion, violently
led the Romans to liberty; Augustus, a scheming tyrant,[7]
conducted them gently to servitude. Under Sulla, while the
republic regained its strength, everyone cried out against the
tyranny; and while tyranny fortified itself under Augustus,
people spoke of nothing but liberty.

The custom of triumphs, which had contributed so much
to Rome's greatness, disappeared under Augustus; or, rather,
this honor became a privilege of sovereignty.[8] Most of the
things that happened under the emperors had their origin in
the republic,[9] and it is necessary to make comparisons. Only
the man under whose auspices a war was undertaken [10] had
the right to claim a triumph; but war was always undertaken
under the auspices of the supreme commander and thus of
the emperor, who was the supreme commander of all the
armies.

In the days of the republic, the principle was to make
war continually; under the emperors, the maxim was to
maintain peace. Victories were regarded as occasions for
worry, involving armies that could set too high a price on
their services.

Those in positions of command feared undertaking things
that were too great. One's glory had to be kept moderate in
order to arouse the attention but not the jealousy of the

prince and to refrain from appearing before him with a bril-
liance his eyes could not tolerate.

Augustus was quite cautious in granting the right of
Roman citizenship; [11] he made laws [12] to prevent the excessive
manumission of slaves.[13] In his will he recommended that
these two policies be adhered to, and that no attempt be
made to extend the empire by new wars.

These three things were clearly linked together: once
there were no more wars, new citizens and manumissions
were no longer necessary.

When Rome was continually engaged in war, it had to
replenish its inhabitants continually. In the beginning, a seg-
ment of the people of each conquered city was led to Rome.
Later, many citizens of neighboring cities came there to share
in the right of voting, and they established themselves in such
large numbers that, on the complaints of the allies, Rome was
often forced to send them back. Finally, crowds came flock-
ing in from the provinces. In addition, the laws favored mar-
riages, and even required them.[c] In all its wars, Rome also
took a prodigious number of slaves, and when its citizens
were loaded with wealth, they bought slaves everywhere. But
slaveowners were moved by generosity, avarice and weakness
of character to free countless numbers of them,[14] some wanting to recompense faithful slaves, others to receive, in their
name, the grain the republic distributed to poor citizens, and
still others, finally, to have in their funeral procession many
attendants crowned with flowers. Almost all of the people
were freedmen,[15] so that these masters of the world not only
in the beginning but in every age were mainly of servile
origin.

Since the number of common people—almost all freed-

---

[c] This was done by the action of censors (in 403 and 151
B.C.) against bachelors, and under Augustus by the law *Papia
Poppaea*. (Jullian).

men or sons of freedmen—had become inconvenient, they
were formed into colonies and in this way helped assure the
loyalty of the provinces. This made for a circulation of the
men of all nations: Rome received them as slaves and sent
them out as Romans.

On the pretext of some rioting at elections, Augustus
placed a governor and garrison in the city. He made the
legions permanent, stationed them along the frontiers, and
established special funds to pay them. Finally, he decreed that
veterans should receive compensation in money, not lands.[16]

Many bad effects resulted from the distribution of lands
carried on since Sulla's time. The ownership of property by
citizens was rendered insecure. If the soldiers of a cohort
were not located in the same place, they wearied of their
situation, left the lands uncultivated, and became dangerous
citizens.[17] But if the lands were distributed by legions, ambitious men could raise armies against the republic at a
moment's notice.

Augustus made fixed provisions for the navy. Just as,
before him, the Romans had lacked permanent land forces,
so too had they lacked permanent sea forces. The main purpose of Augustus' fleets was to provide for the security of
convoys and the communication of the various parts of the
empire with each other. For otherwise the Romans were
masters of the whole Mediterranean, which was the only sea
navigated in those times, and they had no enemy to fear.

Dio quite aptly remarks [d] that under the emperors it was
more difficult to write history. Everything became secret. All
dispatches from the provinces were carried into the emperors'
cabinet. Nothing more was known than what the folly and
boldness of tyrants did not wish to conceal, or what historians conjectured.

---

[d] (Dio, LIII, 19.)

NOTES

1. In our day, almost all those who condemned Charles I came to a tragic end. This is because such actions can scarcely be performed without making mortal enemies on all sides and thus without risking endless danger.
2. The Abbé de Saint-Réal.
3. See Dio, LI (9).
4. There were no garrisons in the cities to restrain them, and the Romans had not needed to secure their empire by anything but armies or colonies.
5. This is quite obvious in the *Letters of Cicero to Atticus*.
6. Caesar made war on the Gauls, and Crassus on the Parthians, without any deliberation by the senate or decree by the people. See Dio (XXXVIII, 31; XL, 12).
7. I use this word here as it was used by the Greeks and Romans, who gave the name to everyone who had overthrown a democracy.
8. Only the triumphal ornaments were now given to individuals. Dio, *Augustus* (LIV, 24).
9. Since the Romans had changed their government without being invaded, their customs remained the same, and even the form of their government remained much the same.
10. Dio, *Augustus,* LIV (11, 24), says that Agrippa's modesty kept him from giving the senate an account of his expedition against the peoples of the Bosporus, that he even refused a triumph, and that no general triumphed thereafter. But this was a favor Augustus wanted to grant Agrippa and which Antony did not grant Ventidius the first time he conquered the Parthians.
11. Suetonius, *Augustus* (40).
12. *Ibid.* See the *Institutes*, I (5, 6).
13. Dio, *Augustus* (LV, 13).
14. Dionysius of Halicarnassus, IV (28).
15. See Tacitus, *Annals*, XIII (27): *Late fusum id corpus,* etc. (The freedmen were a large and extensive body.)

16. He determined that the praetorian soldiers would receive five thousand drachmas: two thousand after sixteen years of service, and the other three after twenty years of service. Dio, *Augustus* (LV, 23).

17. See Tacitus, *Annals,* XIV (27), regarding the soldiers taken to Tarentum and Antium.

CHAPTER XIV

TIBERIUS

As a river slowly and silently undermines the dikes erected against it and finally overthrows them in a moment, flooding the countryside they protected, so in the same way the sovereign power that acted insensibly under Augustus overthrew things violently under Tiberius.

There was a *law of majesty* [a] against those who committed some crime against the Roman people. Tiberius seized upon this law and applied it, not to the cases for which it had been made, but to anything that could serve his hatred or suspicion. Not only did actions fall within the scope of this law, but words, signs and even thoughts—for what is said in those outpourings of the heart occasioned by the conversation of two friends can only be regarded as thoughts. Consequently, there no longer was any liberty at banquets, any confidence among kindred, any fidelity in slaves. With the dissimulation and melancholy of the prince spreading everywhere, friendship was regarded as a danger, frankness as impudence, virtue as an affectation that could recall the happiness of earlier times to the mind of the peoples.

---

[a] This was an old law of the republic directed against military treason, sedition, bad administration and all things involving injury to the majesty of the Roman people. The crime of *lese-majesty,* after Tiberius, involved accusations of treason against the emperor.

No tyranny is more cruel than the one practiced in the shadow of the laws and under color of justice—when, so to speak, one proceeds to drown the unfortunate on the very plank by which they had saved themselves.

And since a tyrant never lacks instruments for his tyranny, Tiberius always found judges ready to condemn as many people as he might suspect. In the days of the republic, the senate, which as a body did not judge the cases of individuals, was informed by a delegation of the people of the crimes imputed to allies. In the same way Tiberius referred to it the judgment of everything he called a crime of *lese-majesty* against himself. This body fell into a state of unspeakable baseness. The senators actually sought servitude, and under the patronage of Sejanus, the most illustrious among them practiced the trade of informer.

It seems to me that I see several reasons for the spirit of servitude which then reigned in the senate. After Caesar had vanquished the party of the republic, both his friends and his enemies in the senate agreed to remove all the limits the laws had set to his power and to confer excessive honors upon him. The former sought to please him, the latter to make him odious. Dio tells us [b] that some went so far as to propose that he be permitted to enjoy all the women he pleased. This was the cause of his not distrusting the senate, and brought about his assassination. But it was also the reason, in the following reigns, why there was no act of flattery lacking a precedent or capable of revolting the mind.

Before Rome was governed by one man, the riches of the leading Romans were immense, whatever the means employed to acquire them. Almost all these riches were taken away under the emperors. The senators no longer had great clients who heaped wealth upon them, and in the provinces little could be taken except for Caesar, especially once his

---

[b] (Dio, XLIV, 7.)

procurators, who were almost like our intendants today, were
established there. But even though the source of riches was
cut off, expenses remained constant; the course of life was
set, and only the emperor's favor could now sustain it.

Augustus had taken the power of making laws and judging public crimes away from the people, but he had left them,
or at least had seemed to leave them, the power of electing the
magistrates. Tiberius, who feared the assemblies of so numerous a people, took away even this privilege and gave it to
the senate—that is, to himself.[1] Now it is hardly credible
to what extent this decline of the people's power debased the
souls of the great. When the people disposed of dignities, the
magistrates who solicited them did many base things. But
these were joined to, and hidden by, a certain magnificence
displayed in the games or meals they gave the people, or the
money or grain they distributed. Although the motive was
base, the means had something noble about them because it
is always fitting for a great man to obtain the favor of the
people by his liberality. But when the people no longer had
anything to give, and the prince, in the name of the senate,
disposed of all offices, the latter were sought and obtained
by contemptible means. Flattery, infamy, and crime were the
arts necessary for success.

It does not appear, however, that Tiberius wanted to
degrade the senate. He complained of nothing so much as the
inclination of this body to servitude; all his life he expressed
disgust with it. But like most men he wanted contradictory
things; his general policy was not in accord with his personal
passions. He would have desired a senate that was free and
capable of winning respect for his government, but he also
wanted a senate which at every moment satisfied his fears,
jealousies, and hatreds. In short, the statesman yielded continually to the man.

We have said that the people had formerly gotten the
patricians to concede them plebeian magistrates who would

defend them against the insults and injustices they might
receive. In order that these magistrates might be in a position
to exercise this power, they were declared sacred and inviolable, and it was decreed that whoever mistreated a tribune
by deed or word would immediately be punished by death.
Now once the emperors were vested with the power of the
tribunes, they obtained their privileges. And it is on this
basis that so many men were put to death, that informers
could ply their trade with complete ease, and that the charge
of lese-majesty—the crime of those to whom no crime can be
imputed, as Pliny says[c]—was extended to cover whatever
one wished.

I believe, however, that some of these grounds of accusa-
tion were not as ridiculous as they appear to us today. I cannot think that Tiberius would have indicted a man for
having sold a statue of the emperor with his house, that
Domitian would have condemned a woman to death for having disrobed before his image, and a citizen because he had
a picture of the whole earth painted on the walls of his room,
if these actions had only aroused in the mind of the Romans
the idea they convey to us at present. I believe this is partly
explained by Rome's having changed government, so that
what does not appear to us to be of any consequence may
have been so then. I judge by what we see today in a nation
that cannot be suspected of tyranny, where it is forbidden to
drink to the health of a certain person.[d]

I cannot overlook anything that serves to reveal the genius
of the Roman people. So thoroughly accustomed were they
to obeying and to making their happiness depend completely
on the difference between one master and another, that after
the death of Germanicus they gave evidence of mourning,

---

[c] Pliny the Younger (*Panegyric,* XLII).

[d] This is an allusion to the prohibition in England after 1688 against
drinking to the health of the Stuart pretenders.

regret, and despair such as could never be found among us. It is necessary to see how the historians describe so great, so long, and so immoderate a public desolation.[2] Nor was it feigned, for the whole body of the people does not pretend, flatter or dissimulate.

Since the Roman people no longer took part in the government, and were almost all freedmen, or men without an occupation who lived at the expense of the public treasury, they were conscious of nothing but their impotence. They grieved like children and women, who are distressed by their feeling of weakness. They were ill. They set their fears and hopes on the person of Germanicus, and when this was snatched from them they fell into despair.

No people fear unhappiness so much as those who ought to be reassured by the wretchedness of their condition, and who should say, with Andromache [e]: *May God let me fear!* In Naples today there are fifty thousand men who live on herbs alone, and have as their sole possession only half a cotton garment. These people, the most unhappy on earth, fall into frightful despondency at the slightest smoke from Vesuvius. They are foolish enough to fear becoming unhappy.

NOTES

1. Tacitus, *Annals,* I (15); Dio, LIV (6).
2. See Tacitus (*Annals,* II, 82).

---

[e] See Seneca's *Troades,* Act III, 630 ff.

CHAPTER XV

THE EMPERORS FROM CAIUS
CALIGULA TO ANTONINUS

Caligula succeeeded Tiberius. It was said of him that
there had never been a better slave, nor a more wicked master.
These two things are closely connected, for the same turn of
mind causing a man to be strongly impressed by the unlimited
power of the person in command, causes him to be no less
impressed when he is in command himself.

Caligula reestablished the comitia [1] which Tiberius had
done away with and abolished the arbitrary crime of lese-
majesty which he had established. From this we may judge
that the beginning of the reign of bad princes is often like
the end of the reign of good ones. What good princes do
from virtue, bad ones can do from a desire to run counter
to the conduct of their predecessor. And to this spirit of
contrariety we owe many good regulations, and many bad
ones as well.

What was gained thereby? Caligula did away with accusations for crimes of lese-majesty, but he used his military
powers to put to death all those who displeased him. And
he was not ill-disposed toward just a few senators; he held
a sword suspended over the whole senate, which he threatened
with complete extermination.

This frightful tyranny of the emperors derived from the

general spirit of the Romans. Since the Romans fell under an arbitrary government suddenly, with almost no interval between their commanding and their serving, they were not at all prepared for the change by a moderation of their manners. Their fierce humor remained; the citizens were treated as they themselves had treated conquered enemies, and were governed according to the same plan. The Sulla who entered Rome was no different from the Sulla who entered Athens: he applied the same law of nations. As for states that have been brought under subjection only by imperceptible degrees, when the laws fail them they are still governed by their manners.

The constant sight of gladiators in combat made the Romans extremely fierce. It was observed that Claudius became more inclined to shed blood by seeing spectacles of this kind. The example of this emperor, who was of a gentle nature yet committed so many cruelties, makes it obvious that the education of his time was different from ours.

Since the Romans were accustomed to making sport of human nature in the person of their children and their slaves,[2] they could scarcely know the virtue we call humanity. Can the ferocity we find in the inhabitants of our colonies come from anything but the punishments constantly inflicted on this unhappy portion of the human race? When we are cruel in the civil state,[a] what can we expect from natural gentleness and justice?

It is wearying, in the history of the emperors, to see the infinite number of men they put to death for the purpose of confiscating their wealth. We find nothing similar in our modern histories. This, as we have just said, must be attrib-

---

[a] The term "civil state" means civil or political society as distinguished from man's natural condition or the "state of nature." The distinction is adopted from Hobbes and Locke: see Montesquieu's *The Spirit of the Laws*, I, 2, 3.

uted to gentler manners, and to a more repressive religion. Moreover, we do not have for despoiling the families of senators who had ravaged the world. The advantages we draw from the moderate size of our fortunes is that they are more secure: it is not worth anyone's trouble to plunder our wealth.[3]

The people of Rome, who were called *plebs,* did not hate the worst emperors. After they had lost their power, and were no longer occupied with war, they had become the vilest of all peoples. They regarded commerce and the arts as things fit for slaves, and the distributions of grain that they received made them neglect the land. They had been accustomed to games and spectacles. When they no longer had tribunes to listen to or magistrates to elect, these useless things became necessities, and idleness increased their taste for them. Thus Caligula, Nero, Commodus, and Caracalla were lamented by the people because of their very madness, for they wildly loved what the people loved, and contributed with all their power and even their persons to the people's pleasures. For them these rulers were prodigal of all the riches of the empire, and when these were exhausted, the people—looking on untroubled while all the great families were being despoiled—enjoyed the fruits of the tyranny. And their joy was pure, for they found security in their own baseness. Such princes naturally hated good men: they knew they were not approved of by them.[4] Indignant at meeting contradiction or silence from an austere citizen, intoxicated by the plaudits of the populace, they succeeded in imagining that their government produced public felicity, and that only ill-intentioned men could censure it.

Caligula was a true sophist in his cruelty. Since he was descended from both Antony and Augustus, he said he would punish the consuls both if they celebrated the day of rejoicing established in memory of the victory of Actium, and if they did not celebrate it. And when Drusilla, to whom he accorded divine honors, died, it was both a crime to mourn her, because she was a goddess, and not to mourn her, because she was his sister.

This is the place to set before ourselves the spectacle of things human. How many wars do we see undertaken in the history of Rome, how much blood shed, how many peoples destroyed, how many great actions, how many triumphs, how much statecraft, how much sobriety, prudence, constancy, and courage! But how did this project for invading all nations end—a project so well planned, carried out and completed— except by satiating the happiness of five or six monsters? What! This senate had brought about the extinction of so many kings only to fall into the meanest enslavement to some of its most contemptible citizens, and to exterminate itself by its own decrees! We build up our power only to see it the better overturned! Men labor to increase their power only to see it fall into more fortunate hands and turned against themselves!

After Caligula had been killed, the senate assembled to establish a form of government. While it was deliberating, some soldiers entered the palace to pillage it. In an obscure place they found a man trembling with fear. It was Claudius: they acclaimed him emperor.

Claudius completed the ruin of the old orders by giving his officers the right to dispense justice.[5] The wars of Marius and Sulla were principally waged to determine just who would have this right, the senators or the knights.[6] An imbecile's fancy took it away from both—strange outcome of a dispute that had set the whole world aflame!

No authority is more absolute than that of a prince who succeeds a republic, for he finds himself with all the power of the people, who had not been able to impose limitations on themselves. Thus we see the kings of Denmark today exercising the most arbitrary power in Europe.

The people were no less debased than the senate and

knights. We have seen that, until the time of the emperors, they had been so warlike that the armies raised in the city were disciplined on the spot and went straight to the enemy. In the civil wars of Vitellius and Vespasian, Rome became a prey to every ambitious man, and, full of timid *bourgeois*, trembled before the first band of soldiers to approach it.

The condition of the emperors was no better. Since the right or the daring to elect an emperor was not confined to a single army, it was enough for someone to be elected by one army for him to be displeasing to the others, who at once named a competitor.

Thus, just as the greatness of the republic was fatal to its republican government, so the greatness of the empire was fatal to the lives of the emperors. If they had had a country of only moderate size to defend, they would have had only one main army, which, having once elected them, would have respected its own handiwork.

The soldiers had been attached to the family of Caesar, who was the guarantee of all the advantages the revolution had procured for them. The time came when the great families of Rome were all exterminated by Caesar's family, and when, in the person of Nero, it too perished. The civil power, which had been steadily beaten down, was in no position to counterbalance the military; each army wanted to create an emperor.

At this point let us compare different periods. When Tiberius began to reign, he made most advantageous use of the senate.[7] He learned that the Roman armies in Illyria and Germany had revolted. He granted some of their demands, maintained that it was for the senate to judge the others,[8] and sent them deputies from this body. Those who no longer fear power can still respect authority. When the rebellious soldiers were shown that, within a Roman army, the lives of the emperor's children and the senate's envoys were in danger,[9] they were capable of repenting and went so far as to punish themselves.[10] But when the senate was completely downtrodden, its example moved no one. Otho harangued his soldiers in vain to tell them of the senate's dignity;[11] in vain did Vitellius send the principal senators to make peace with Vespasian for him.[12] The respect which has been taken away from the orders of the state for so long cannot be restored at a moment's notice. The armies only regarded these deputies as the most cowardly slaves of a master they had already condemned.

It was an old custom of the Romans that whoever enjoyed a triumph distributed a few denarii[b] to each soldier; it was very little.[13] In the civil wars these gifts were increased.[14] Formerly they consisted of money taken from the enemy; in these unhappy times it was the money of citizens, and the soldiers wanted a share even where there had been no booty. These distributions had taken place only after war; Nero used them during peace. The soldiers grew accustomed to them; and they were enraged at Galba, who courageously told them that he knew how to choose soldiers but not how to buy them.

Galba, Otho,[15] and Vitellius were only briefly in power. Like them, Vespasian was elected by the soldiers. In the course of his whole reign he thought only of reestablishing the empire, which had been successively occupied by six tyrants equally cruel, almost all wild, often imbecile, and, to make matters worse, prodigal to the point of madness.

Titus, who succeeded him, was the delight of the Roman people. Domitian revealed himself a new monster who was more cruel or at least more implacable than his predecessors because he was more timorous.

Seeing that he was as dangerous in his friendships as in his hatreds, and that he placed no limits on either his suspicions or his accusations, his favorite freedmen and—as some

---

[b] The denarius was a silver coin valued at ten asses. See the discussion of the soldiers' regular pay in Chapter XVI.

have said—his wife herself, got rid of him. Before striking the blow they looked around for a successor, and chose Nerva, a venerable old man.

Nerva adopted Trajan, the most accomplished prince in the annals of history. It was a blessing to be born in his reign; nothing was so fortunate or so glorious for the great Roman people. He was a great statesman and a great general. He had a good heart, which inclined him toward the good, an enlightened mind which taught him what was best, and a soul that was noble, great, and beautiful. He possessed all the virtues without being extreme in any, and was, in short, the man most suitable for honoring human nature and representing the divine.

He executed Caesar's project and warred against the Parthians successfully. Any other man would have succumbed in an enterprise where the dangers were immediate and the resources distant, where it was absolutely necessary to conquer, and where there was no assurance of survival after conquering.

The difficulty consisted both in the situation of the two empires and in the style of warfare of the two peoples. What if one took the road through Armenia, toward the sources of the Tigris and Euphrates? One found a mountainous and difficult country where convoys could not be led, so that the army would be half ruined before arriving in Media.[16] What if one entered at a lower point, toward the south, through Nisibis? [c] One found a dreadful desert that separated the two empires. What if one wished to pass lower still, and go through Mesopotamia? One traversed a country that was partly uncultivated, partly submerged. And with the Tigris and Euphrates going from north to south, one could not penetrate into the country without leaving the rivers, and could hardly leave the rivers without perishing.

---

[c] Nisibis: a city in northern Mesopotamia.

As to the style of warfare of the two nations, the strength of the Romans consisted in their infantry—the strongest, most steadfast and best disciplined in the world.

The Parthians had no infantry but an admirable cavalry. They fought from afar, and beyond the range of Roman arms. The javelin could rarely reach them. Their arms were bows and fearful arrows, and they rather besieged an army than engaged it in combat. They were pursued in vain because, for them, to flee was to fight. They made their peoples withdraw as the enemy approached, leaving only garrisons in the strongholds; and when these were taken, they had to be destroyed. They skillfully burned the whole countryside around the enemy army, and deprived it of the very grass. In short, they made war in much the same way it is still made today along the same frontiers.

Moreover, the legions of Illyria and Germany, which were transferred into this war, were not suitable for it.[17] Accustomed in their own country to eating heavily, the soldiers perished almost to the last man.

Thus, the Parthians did what no nation had yet done and avoided the Roman yoke—not by being invincible, but by being inaccessible.

Hadrian abandoned Trajan's conquests,[18] and set the bounds of the empire at the Euphrates. And it is admirable that after so many wars the Romans should have lost only what they had wanted to give up—like the sea, which diminishes only when it withdraws by itself.

Hadrian's conduct caused many murmurs. In the sacred books of the Romans, people read that when Tarquin wanted to build the Capitol he found the most suitable place already occupied by the statues of many other divinities. With his knowledge of augury he inquired if they would be willing to cede their place to Jupiter. All consented, with the exception of Mars, Youth, and the god Terminus.[19] This gave rise to three religious opinions: that the people of Mars would cede the area they occupied to no one; that the Roman youth would never be overcome; and, finally, that the Roman god Terminus would never move back—all of which did happen, however, under Hadrian.

NOTES

1. He abolished them subsequently.
2. See the Roman laws on the power of fathers and masters.
3. The duke of Braganza had immense properties in Portugal; when he rebelled, the king of Spain was congratulated on the rich confiscation he was going to obtain.
4. The Greeks had games in which it was a proper thing to fight, as it was a glorious thing to win. The Romans had little else but spectacles; and that of the infamous gladiators was peculiar to them. Now Roman gravity would not suffer a great person to descend into the arena or step on the stage himself. How could a senator bring himself to do such a thing, he whom the laws forbade to contract any alliance with those blemished by the disapproval or even the applause of the people? Emperors appeared there, however; and this folly, which gave evidence of the most extreme corruption of the heart, and a scorn for what was beautiful, upright and good, is always stamped by the historians with the character of tyranny.
5. Augustus had established the procurators, but they had no judicial power, and when they were disobeyed they had to have recourse to the authority of the governor of the province, or of the praetor. But, under Claudius, they obtained ordinary judicial powers, as provincial lieutenants; they judged even fiscal affairs, which put everyone's fortunes in their hands.
6. See Tacitus, *Annals,* XII (60).
7. Tacitus, *Annals,* I (6).
8. *Caetera senatui servanda* (The other demands must be reserved for the senate). Tacitus, *Annals,* I (25).
9. See Germanicus' harangue. Tacitus, *Annals,* I (42).

10. *Gaudebat caedibus miles, quasi semet absolveret* (And the troops rejoiced in the slaughter, as if it absolved them of their own guilt). Tacitus, *Annals,* I (44). Afterwards the extorted privileges were revoked.

11. Tacitus, *History,* I (84).

12. Tacitus, *History,* III (80).

13. See, in Livy, the sums distributed at various triumphs. The generals were disposed to bring much money into the public treasury and to give little of it to the soldiers.

14. At a time when the size of conquests had caused gifts to increase, Paulus Aemilius distributed only a hundred denarii to each soldier. But Caesar gave two thousand, and his example was followed by Antony and Octavius, and by Brutus and Cassius. See Dio (XLIII, 22), and Appian.

15. *Suscepere duo manipulares imperium populi Romani transferendum, et transtulerunt* (Two common soldiers thus undertook to transfer the imperium of the Roman people, and they did so). Tacitus, *History,* I (25).

16. The country did not furnish enough large trees to make machines for besieging strongholds. Plutarch, *Life of Antony* (38).

17. See Herodian, *Life of Alexander Severus* (VI).

18. See Eutropius (VIII). Dacia was abandoned only under Aurelian.

19. Saint Augustine, *The City of God,* IV, 23, 29.

CHAPTER XVI

THE CONDITION OF THE EMPIRE,

FROM ANTONINUS

TO PROBUS

At that time the Stoic sect [a] was expanding and gaining favor in the empire. It seemed that human nature had made an effort to produce this admirable sect out of itself—like those plants the earth brings forth in places the heavens have never seen.

The Romans owed their best emperors to it. Nothing can make us forget the first Antoninus except the man he adopted—Marcus Aurelius. We feel a secret pleasure within ourselves in speaking of this emperor; we cannot read his life without experiencing a kind of tenderness. Such is the effect it produces that we have a better opinion of ourselves because we have a better opinion of men.

The wisdom of Nerva, the glory of Trajan, the valor of

---

[a] Stoicism originated with Zeno in Athens in the third century B.C. It was introduced at Rome by Panaetius toward the middle of the second century B.C., and later received support from the teachings of Seneca, Epictetus and Marcus Aurelius. Its stress was moral, and its central tenet was that virtue constituted not only the highest but the sole good for man.

Hadrian, and the virtue of the two Antonines commanded the respect of the soldiers. But, when new monsters took their place, the abuses of military government appeared in all their excesses; and the soldiers, who had sold the empire, assassinated the emperors in order to obtain a new price for it.

We hear that somewhere in the world a prince [b] has been working for fifteen years to abolish civil government in his states and establish military government. I have no wish to make odious reflections on this design. I shall only say that, by the nature of things, two hundred guards can give security to the life of a prince, but not eighty thousand; besides which, it is more dangerous to oppress an armed people than one that is not armed.

Commodus succeeded Marcus Aurelius, his father. He was a monster who indulged all his passions and all those of his ministers and courtesans. Those who rid the world of him put in his place a venerable old man named Pertinax, whom the praetorian guards immediately massacred.

They put the empire up for auction, and Didius Julianus won it with his promises. Everyone was indignant at this, for although the empire had been bought before, it had never been haggled over. Pescennius Niger, Severus, and Albinus were acclaimed emperors; and Julianus was abandoned by the soldiers because he could not pay the immense sums he had promised.

Severus defeated Niger and Albinus. He had great qualities, but gentleness—that prime virtue of princes—was lacking in him.

The power of the emperors could more easily appear tyrannical than the power of the princes of our own day. Their office was a collection of all the Roman magistracies.

---

[b] Probably a reference to Frederick William I, king of Prussia (1713-40 A.D.).

As dictators under the name of emperors, as tribunes of the people, proconsuls, censors, grand pontiffs, and—when they wished—consuls, they often dispensed distributive justice.[c] They could therefore easily arouse the suspicion that they had oppressed those they had condemned—for the people usually judge the abuse of power by the greatness of power. But the kings of Europe, who are legislators and not executors of the law, princes and not judges, have divested themselves of the part of authority that can be odious. And while granting favors themselves, they have committed to special magistrates the meting out of punishments.

Hardly any emperors were more jealous of their authority than Tiberius and Severus. Yet both let themselves be governed in a contemptible fashion, the one by Sejanus, the other by Plautian.

The unfortunate practice of proscription, introduced by Sulla, continued under the emperors; and it was even necessary for a prince to possess some virtue in order not to follow it. For his ministers and favorites immediately envisioned a vast number of confiscations, and they spoke to him only of the need for punishing and the perils of clemency.

The proscriptions of Severus caused many of Niger's soldiers [1] to take refuge among the Parthians.[2] They taught the Parthians what was lacking in their military art, including the use of Roman arms and even their manufacture. Because of this, these peoples, who had usually been content to defend themselves, afterwards were almost always aggressors.[3]

---

[c] Distributive justice is another term here for penal justice. Aristotle originally used it, however, to refer to the distribution of the good things (such as honors, wealth and office) that the public gives out, and only by implication to the burdens that must be shared; as for criminal punishments, they came more under the heading of reciprocal than distributive justice. Compare *Ethics,* V, 2 (end) with V, 5 (beginning).

In this series of civil wars which arose continually, it is remarkable that those who had the support of the European legions almost always vanquished those supported by the Asian legions.[4] And we find in the history of Severus that he could not take the city of Atra in Arabia because the European legions had mutinied, forcing him to use those of Syria.

This difference was evident ever since troop levies were begun in the provinces;[5] and it existed among legions as among peoples themselves, who, by nature and education, are unequally suited for war.

These levies made in the provinces had another effect. Since the emperors were usually drawn from the army, they were nearly all foreigners and sometimes barbarians. Rome was no longer master of the world, but it received laws from the entire world.

Each emperor brought to it something from his country, whether by way of manners, morals, public order, or religion. And Heliogabalus went so far as to want to destroy all of Rome's objects of veneration and remove all the gods from their temples in order to place his own there.

Apart from the secret means God chose to use and which He alone knows, this did much for the establishment of the Christian religion. For there was no longer anything foreign in the empire, and people were prepared to accept all the customs an emperor might wish to introduce.

We know the Romans accepted the gods of other countries into their city. They accepted them as conquerors, and had them carried in the triumphs; but when foreigners themselves came to establish their gods, they were repressed at once. We know, moreover, that the Romans had the custom of giving foreign gods the names of those of their own gods who were most closely related to them. But when the priests of other countries wanted to have their gods worshiped at Rome under their own names, they were not permitted to do so; and this was one of the great obstacles the Christian religion encountered.

Caracalla could be called the destroyer of men rather than a tyrant. Caligula, Nero, and Domitian limited their cruelties to Rome; Caracalla proceeded to extend his frenzy to the whole world.

Severus had employed the exactions of a long reign and the proscriptions of those who had belonged to the party of his competitors to amass immense treasures.

Having begun his reign by killing his brother, Geta, with his own hand, Caracalla used these riches to persuade the soldiers to tolerate his crime; for they loved Geta and said they had taken an oath to both children of Severus, not to one alone.

The treasures amassed by princes almost never have anything but grievous effects. They corrupt the prince's successor, who is dazzled by them; and if they do not corrupt his heart, they corrupt his mind. He immediately plans great enterprises with a power that is accidental, that cannot endure, that is not natural, and that is inflated rather than enlarged.

Caracalla increased the pay of the soldiers. Macrinus wrote the senate that this increase came to seventy million [6] drachmas.[7] It appears this prince exaggerated. If we compare the expense of paying our soldiers today with the rest of the public expenses, and follow the same proportion for the Romans, we see that this sum would have been enormous.

It is necessary to inquire what the pay of the Roman soldier was. We learn from Orosius that Domitian increased the established pay by one quarter.[8] It appears from the speech of a soldier in Tacitus [9] that at Augustus' death it was ten ounces of copper. We find in Suetonius [10] that Caesar had doubled the pay in his time. Pliny [11] says that in the Second Punic War it had been reduced by a fifth. It was therefore about six ounces of copper in the First [12] Punic War, five ounces in the Second,[13] ten under Caesar, and thirteen and a third under Domitian.[14] Here I shall present some reflections.

The pay the republic easily provided when it was only a small state, waged a war every year, and every year received spoils, it could not—without incurring debt—keep up during the First Punic War, when it extended its arms beyond Italy and had to sustain a long war and support large armies.

In the Second Punic War the pay was reduced to five ounces of copper; and this decrease could be effected without danger, at a time when most of the citizens blushed to accept payment at all and wanted to serve at their own expense.

The treasures of Perseus and so many other kings that were continually brought to Rome put an end to taxes there.[15] Amid public and private opulence, the Romans had the wisdom not to increase the pay of five ounces of copper.

Although from this pay a deduction was made for grain, clothing, and arms, it was sufficient because only citizens who had a patrimony were enrolled.

After Marius had enrolled men without a patrimony, and because his example was followed, Caesar was forced to increase the pay.

Since this increase was continued after Caesar's death, the government was compelled, under the consulate of Hirtius and Pansa, to reestablish taxes.

When Domitian's weakness made him increase the pay by a quarter, he dealt a great blow to the state, for the prevalence of luxury—while not itself a misfortune—becomes one if it occurs under conditions which, by the nature of things, call for having only physical necessities. Finally, once Caracalla had granted a new increase, the empire was placed in a situation where it could not endure without soldiers and could not endure with them.

To diminish the horror at the murder of his brother, Caracalla placed him in the rank of the gods, and, oddly enough, this was the treatment he himself received from Macrinus. After having had him stabbed, Macrinus wanted to appease the praetorian guards, who had become desperate at the death of a prince who had given them so much. He had a temple built to him and established flaminian priests [d] in his honor.

This was why Caracalla's memory was not stigmatized, and why, since the senate did not dare judge him, he was not placed in the rank of the tyrants, like Commodus, who did not deserve it more than he.[16]

Of two great emperors, Hadrian and Severus,[17] one established military discipline, and the other relaxed it. The effects correspond directly to the causes: the reigns following Hadrian's were happy and tranquil; those following Severus full of horrors.

The gifts Caracalla lavished on the soldiers had been immense; and he had very faithfully followed his dying father's counsel to enrich the military and not bother about anyone else.

But this policy could hardly be good for more than one reign. The succeeding emperor, unable to maintain the same expenses, was immediately massacred by the army, so that the wise emperors were always put to death by the soldiers, and the wicked ones by the plots or decrees of the senate.

When a tyrant gave himself over to the military and left the citizens exposed to its violence and rapine, the situation could not last more than one reign; for the soldiers, by their destruction, went so far as to strip themselves of the sources of their own pay. It therefore became necessary to think of reestablishing military discipline—an enterprise which always cost the life of whoever dared attempt it.

When Caracalla had been killed in a trap laid by Mac-

---

[d] Flaminian priests or *flamines* were those tending particular gods, including deified emperors.

rinus, the soldiers were desperate at having lost a prince who
dispensed without limit, and elected Heliogabalus.[18] The
latter, occupied only with his obscene pleasures, let them live
as they fancied; and when they could no longer tolerate him,
they massacred him. In the same way they killed Alexander,
who wanted to reestablish discipline and spoke of punishing
them.[19]

Thus a tyrant, who made sure not of his life but of his
power to commit crimes, perished with the grievous advantage
that anyone wishing to do better would perish after him.

After Alexander, Maximin, the first emperor of barbarian
origin, was elected. His gigantic height and his physical
strength had made him well known.

He and his son were killed by the soldiers. The first two
Gordians perished in Africa. Maximus, Balbinus, and the
third Gordian were massacred. Philip, who had had the young
Gordian killed, was himself killed with his son; and Decius,
who was elected in his place, perished in turn by the treason
of Gallus.[20]

What was called the Roman empire, in this century, was
a kind of irregular republic, much like the aristocracy of
Algeria, where the army, which has sovereign power, makes
and unmakes a magistrate called the dey. And perhaps it is a
rather general rule that military government is, in certain
respects, republican rather than monarchical.

And let it not be said that the soldiers took part in the
government only by their disobedience and revolts. Did not
the harangues the emperors delivered to them belong, in the
last analysis, to the genre of those the consuls and tribunes
had formerly delivered to the people? And although the
armies did not have one particular place in which to assemble,
although they did not conduct themselves according to certain
forms, although they were not usually coolheaded—being
given to little deliberation and much action—did they not
as sovereigns dispose of the public estate? And what was an

emperor except the minister of a violent government, elected for the special benefit of the soldiers?

When the army made Philip a partner in the imperial power,[21] he was the praetorian prefect of the third Gordian. The latter asked that the entire command be left in his hands, but could not get it. He harangued the army to make them both equal in power, and did not succeed in that either. He begged that the title of Caesar be left to him, and was refused. He asked to be praetorian prefect, and his entreaties were rejected. Finally, he spoke for his life. In its various judgments here, the army was exercising the supreme magistracy.

The barbarians, who at first were unknown to the Romans, then only inconvenient, had become dangerous to them. By the most extraordinary set of circumstances, Rome had so completely annihilated all peoples that, when Rome itself was conquered, it seemed that the earth had given birth to new peoples to destroy it.

The princes of great states usually have few neighboring countries that can become the object of their ambition. If any had existed, they would already have been enveloped in the course of conquest. Such states are therefore bounded by seas, mountains, and vast deserts, the destitution of which causes them to be scorned. Thus, the Romans left the Germans in their forests, and the people of the north in their icefields; and nations were preserved, or even formed, there by which the Romans themselves were finally subjugated.

In Gallus' reign, a great number of nations which afterwards became better known ravaged Europe; and the Persians, after invading Syria, only forsook their conquests to preserve their booty.

These swarms of barbarians who once came out of the north no longer appear today. The violence of the Romans had made the peoples of the south withdraw to the north. While the force containing them lasted, they stayed there;

when it was weakened, they spread out in every direction.[22] The same thing happened several centuries later. The conquests of Charlemagne and his tyrannical acts had made the peoples of the south retreat to the north a second time, and as soon as this empire was weakened, they moved from north to south a second time. And if some prince committed the same ravages in Europe today, the nations repulsed to the north, backed against the limits of the world, would hold firm there until the moment when they would inundate and conquer Europe a third time.

As the terrible disorder in the succession to the empire reached its height, one saw thirty different pretenders appear at the end of Valerian's reign and during that of his son, Gallienus. They destroyed each other, for the most part, after very short reigns, and were proclaimed tyrants.

With Valerian captured by the Persians, and his son neglecting affairs, the barbarians penetrated everywhere. The empire found itself in the same condition as it did about a century later in the west,[23] and it would have been destroyed then and there had not a happy concurrence of circumstances given it new life.

Odaenathus, prince of Palmyra—an ally of the Romans —drove back the Persians, who had invaded almost all of Asia. The city of Rome created an army of its citizens which warded off the barbarians who came to pillage it. An immense army of Scythians, which crossed the sea with six thousand vessels, perished from shipwreck, wretched conditions, famine and its own size. And after Gallienus was killed, Claudius, Aurelian, Tacitus, and Probus—four great men, who, by a great stroke of luck, succeeded each other— reestablished an empire that was about to perish.

NOTES

1. Herodian, *Life of Severus* (III, 4).
2. The evil continued under Alexander. Artaxeres, who re-established the Persian empire, became a formidable threat to the Romans because their soldiers—either through caprice or licentiousness—deserted to him in flocks. Xiphilinus' *Abridgement* of Dio, LXXX (3).
3. That is to say, the Persians who came after them.
4. Severus defeated the Asiatic legions of Niger, Constantine those of Licinius. Although he was proclaimed by the armies of Syria, Vespasian made war on Vitellius with the legions of Moesia, Pannonia and Dalmatia only. Cicero, when he was a governor, wrote the senate that levies made in Asia could not be relied upon. Zosimus tells us that Constantine vanquished Maxentius with his cavalry alone. On this point, see the seventh paragraph in Chapter XXII of this work.
5. Augustus made the legions permanent bodies, and placed them in the provinces. In early times, levies were only raised in Rome, then among the Latins, later in Italy, and finally in the provinces.
6. Seven thousand myriads. Dio, *Macrinus* (LXXVIII, 6).
7. The Attic drachma was the Roman denarius—an eighth of an ounce and a sixty-fourth of our mark.
8. He increased it in the proportion of seventy-five to a hundred.
9. *Annals,* I (17).
10. *Life of Caesar* (XXVI).
11. *Natural History,* XXXIII, art. 13. Instead of giving ten ounces of copper for twenty, they gave sixteen.
12. A soldier in Plautus' *Mostellaria* says that it was three *asses* —which can only mean *asses* of two ounces. But if the pay was exactly six ounces of copper during the First Punic War, during the Second it did not diminish by a fifth but by a sixth, and the fraction was disregarded. (See Jullian on the wording of this note.)

13. Polybius, who evaluates it in Greek money, differs only by a fraction (VI, 39).

14. See Orosius, and Suetonius, *Domitian* (7). They say the same thing using different expressions. I have made these reductions to ounces of copper so that the reader need have no knowledge of Roman monies to understand me.

15. Cicero, *Offices,* II (21).

16. Aelius Lampridius, *The Life of Alexander Severus* (9, 10).

17. See the *Life of Hadrian* in Xiphilinus' *Abridgment,* and Herodian's *Life of Severus* (III, 8).

18. In those days everyone believed himself qualified to become emperor. See Dio, LXXIX.

19. See Lampridius (59).

20. Concerning Augustan History, Casaubon remarks that in the one hundred and sixty years it embraces, there were seventy persons who, justly or unjustly, had the title of Caesar: *Adeo erant in illo principatu, quem tamen omnes mirantur, comitia imperii semper incerta* (Under the principate of that period, surprising as it may seem, elections to the throne were still always insecure). This clearly reveals the difference between this government and the government of France, where the kingdom has had only sixty-three kings in twelve hundred years.

21. See Jules Capitolinus (*The Life of Gordian III,* 30).

22. We see what the following famous question reduces to: *Why is the north no longer as populous as it used to be?*

23. One hundred and fifty years later, under Honorius, the barbarians overran it.

CHAPTER XVII

CHANGE IN THE STATE

To forestall the continual treachery of the soldiers, the emperors made partners of persons in whom they had confidence. And on the pretext that the burden of public affairs was too heavy, Diocletian decreed that there should always be two emperors and two Caesars. He judged that the four main armies, in the employ of those who shared in the empire, would stand in fear of each other, and that the other armies, too weak to try making emperors of their own commanders, would gradually lose the habit of electing. He believed, finally, that with the dignity of Caesar being kept subordinate, a power divided in four for the security of the government would still, in its whole extent, be in the hands of two.

But what restrained the military even more was that the riches of individuals and the wealth of the public had diminished, and the emperors could no longer make them such considerable gifts, so that the reward was no longer proportionate to the danger of instituting a new election.

Besides, the praetorian prefects—who in power and function were much like the grand viziers of those days, and had emperors massacred at will in order to put themselves in their place—were much reduced by Constantine. He left them only civil functions, and created four prefects instead of two.

The lives of the emperors began, therefore, to be more secure. They could die in their beds, and that seemed to make

them somewhat gentler in their ways; they no longer shed
blood with such ferocity. But, since this immense power had
to overflow somewhere, another kind of tyranny appeared, but
one that was more muted. It expressed itself not in massacres
but in iniquitous judgments, in forms of justice that seemed
to set aside death only to dishonor life. The court was governed, and itself governed, with more artifice, with more
exquisite arts, and amid greater silence. Finally, boldness in
conceiving an evil action and impetuosity in committing it
disappeared, and only the vices of feeble souls, and calculated
crimes, prevailed in their place.

A new kind of corruption set in. The early emperors loved
pleasures; these, indolence. They made fewer appearances
before the military; they were idler, more under the sway
of their personal entourage, more attached to their palaces,
and more isolated from the empire.

As the court became more isolated, its poisonous influence became more powerful. Nothing was said, everything
insinuated. All great reputations were attacked, and the ministers and military officers were constantly placed at the mercy
of the sort of person who can neither serve the state nor
endure others serving it with glory.[1]

Finally, that affability of the early emperors, which alone
could serve to acquaint them with state affairs, disappeared
entirely. The prince no longer knew anything except on the
report of a few confidants, who—always in concert, often even
when they seemed to be of contrary opinions—served him
as no more than a single individual.

The sojourn of several emperors in Asia, and their perpetual rivalry with the kings of Persia, imbued them with
the desire to be worshiped like the latter; and Diocletian—
others say Galerius—ordered it by an edict.

As this Asiatic ostentation and pomp was being established, people quickly grew accustomed to it. And when
Julian wanted to invest his manners with simplicity and

modesty, what was only reminiscent of the old morals was called neglect of his dignity.

Although after Marcus Aurelius' time there had been several emperors, there had been only one empire. And since the authority of all of them was recognized in the provinces, it was a single power exercised by several men.

But when Galerius and Constantius Chlorus could not agree with each other, they really divided the empire.[2] And by this example—which Constantine later followed, choosing Galerius' plan and not Diocletian's—a practice was introduced that was less a change than a revolution.

Moreover, Constantine's desire to found a new city and his vanity in wanting to give it his name, made him carry the seat of empire to the East. Although the circumference of Rome was not nearly as large as it is now, its suburbs were prodigiously extended.[3] Italy, full of country houses, was nothing but the garden of Rome. The farmers were in Sicily, Africa and Egypt,[4] and the gardeners in Italy; the lands were almost wholly cultivated by the slaves of Roman citizens. But, when the seat of empire was established in the East, almost the whole of Rome went over, the great took their slaves there—which is to say nearly all the people—and Italy was deprived of its inhabitants.

So that the new city would in no way be inferior to the old, Constantine wanted grain to be distributed there too and ordered the grain from Egypt sent to Constantinople and the grain from Africa sent to Rome—which, it seems to me, was not very sensible.

In the time of the Republic, the Roman people, sovereign over all others, naturally had to receive some part of the tributes. This was the reason why the senate at first sold them grain at a low price, and later gave it away for nothing. When the government became monarchical, the practice lasted, though contrary to the principles of monarchy; the abuse was left standing because of the inconvenience that would have been entailed in changing it. But Constantine, founding a new city, established the same practice there for no good reason.

When Augustus had conquered Egypt, he carried the treasure of the Ptolemies to Rome. This caused much the same revolution there that the discovery of the Indies has since caused in Europe, and that certain systems [a] have caused in our own day. Property doubled in price at Rome.[5] And since Rome continued to attract the riches of Alexandria, which itself received those of Africa and the Orient, gold and silver became very common in Europe. This enabled its peoples to pay very considerable taxes in money.

But, with the empire divided, these riches went to Constantinople. We know, besides, that the mines of England were not yet opened;[6] that there were very few of them in Italy and Gaul;[7] that after the time of the Carthaginians, the mines of Spain were hardly worked, or at least were no longer as rich.[8] Italy, with nothing but its abandoned gardens, had no means of attracting the East's money, while the West, to get commodities from the East, sent its money there. Thus, gold and silver became extremely rare in Europe; but the emperors wanted to exact the same tributes as ever, which ruined everything.

When a government's form has been established a long time and things are arranged in a certain way, it is almost always prudent to leave them alone, because the reasons for such a state having endured are often complicated and unknown, and they will cause it to maintain itself further. But when one changes the whole system, one can only remedy those difficulties that are known by theory, and one overlooks others that can only be brought to light by practice.

---

[a] This phrase is probably a reference to the speculative enterprises of John Law.

Thus, although the empire was already too large, the new division ruined it because all the parts of this great body, together so long, had, so to speak, adjusted themselves to remain that way and to depend on each other.

After having weakened the capital, Constantine [9] struck another blow at the frontiers. He removed the legions that were stationed along the banks of the great rivers, and dispersed them within the provinces. This produced two evils: one, that the barrier holding so many nations in check was removed, and the other, that the soldiers [10] lived and grew soft in the circus and theaters. [11]

When Constantius sent Julian to Gaul, he found that fifty cities along the Rhine [12] had been taken by the barbarians, that the provinces had been sacked, and that only the shadow of a Roman army remained, which could be put to flight by the mere name of its enemies.

By his wisdom, constancy, economy, conduct, bravery and a continuous series of heroic actions, this prince drove back the barbarians; [13] and the terror of his name held them in check as long as he lived. [14]

The brevity of reigns in the empire, the various political parties, the different religions, the particular sects of these religions, have caused the character of the emperors to come down to us extremely distorted. I shall give only two examples. The same Alexander who is so cowardly in Herodian appears full of courage in Lampridius; the Gratian who is so highly praised by the orthodox is compared by Philostorgus to Nero.

Valentinian, more than anyone else, sensed the necessity of the old system. He spent his whole life fortifying the banks of the Rhine, making levees, building castles, placing troops there, and giving them the means of subsistence. But the world then witnessed an event that made his brother, Valens, open the Danube, and with frightful consequences.

In the country between the Palus Maeotis,[b] the Caucasian mountains, and the Caspian sea, there were many peoples belonging mostly to the nations of the Huns or Alans. Their lands were extremely fertile; they loved war and brigandage; they were almost always on horseback or on their chariots, and roamed the country in which they were enclosed. They did indeed undertake some ravaging along the frontiers of Persia and Armenia, but the Caspian Gates [c] were easily guarded, and they could penetrate into Persia elsewhere only with difficulty. Since they did not imagine it possible to cross the Palus Maeotis,[15] they were not acquainted with the Romans; and while other barbarians ravaged the empire, they remained within the limits their ignorance set for them.

Some [16] have said that the mud carried by the Tanais had formed a kind of crust on the Cimmerian Bosporus [d] over which they had passed; others,[17] that two young Scythians, pursuing a hind that had crossed this arm of the sea, crossed it also. They were astonished to see a new world; returning to the old, they apprised their compatriots of the new lands, and—if I may be so bold as to use this term—of the Indies they had discovered.[18]

Immediately, countless bodies of Huns passed over, and meeting first with the Goths, drove them along before them. It seemed these nations were precipitating themselves one on the other, and that in order to press upon Europe, Asia had acquired a new weight.

The frightened Goths appeared at the banks of the Danube, and, holding their hands in supplication, begged for refuge. Valens' flatterers seized on this opportunity and

---

[b] Palus Maeotis: the Sea of Azov.

[c] Caspian Gates: a defile in Media between the Greater Caucasus and the Caspian Sea.

[d] Tanais: the Don; Cimmerian Bosporus: the strait between the Sea of Azov and the Black Sea.

represented it to him as the happy conquest of a new people, who came to defend and enrich the empire.[19]

Valens ordered the Goths to cross without arms; but, for money, his officers let them keep whatever arms they wanted.[20] He had lands distributed to them, but, unlike the Huns, the Goths were not farmers.[21] They were even deprived of the grain that was promised them. They were dying of famine, in the midst of a rich country; they were armed, and were being subjected to injustices. They ravaged everything, from the Danube to the Bosporus, exterminated Valens and his army, and only re-crossed the Danube in order to abandon the dreadful solitude they had created.[22]

NOTES

1. See what the authors tell us about the court of Constantine, of Valens, etc.

2. See Orosius, VII (25) and Aurelius Victor.

3. *Expatiantia tecta multas addidere urbes* (The spreading out of buildings has added many cities to it). Pliny, *Natural History*, III (art. 67).

4. "Grain used to be carried from Italy to the remote provinces," says Tacitus, "and Italy is still not sterile; but we cultivate Africa and Egypt instead, and prefer to expose the life of the Roman people to accidents." *Annals*, XII (43).

5. Suetonius, *Augustus* (XLI); *Orosius*, VI (19). Rome had often had such revolutions. I have said that the treasures brought in from Macedonia had put an end to all taxes. *Unius imperatoris praeda finem attulit tributorum* (the booty of one general put an end to taxes forever). Cicero, *Offices*, II (22).

6. Tacitus, *The Manners of the Germans*, says so explicitly. We know, besides, just about when the German mines were opened. See Thomas Sesreiberus on the origin of the Hartz mines. Those of Saxony are believed to be less old.

7. See Pliny, XXXVII, art. 77.

8. Diodorus (V, 36) says that the Carthaginians were highly skilled in the art of exploiting them, and the Romans in preventing others from doing so.

9. What is said here of Constantine does not conflict with the ecclesiastical authors, who declare they intend to cover only those of his actions relating to piety, and not those relating to the government of the state. Eusebius, *Life of Constantine,* I, 9 (11); Socrates, I, 1.

10. Zosimus, VIII (34).

11. After the establishment of Christianity, gladiatorial combats became rare. Constantine forbade them, and they were completely abolished under Honorius, as appears from Theodoret and Otto of Freising. Of their old spectacles, the Romans retained only those that could sap their spirit and that served as an enticement to sensual pleasure.

12. Ammianus Marcellinus, XVI, XVII, XVIII.

13. *Ibid.*

14. See Ammianus Marcellinus' magnificent eulogy of this prince, XXV (3). See also the fragments of John of Antioch's *History.*

15. Procopius, *Miscellaneous History* (*The Gothic War,* IV, 5).

16. Zosimus, IV (20).

17. Jordanes, *Gothic History* (XXIV). Procopius' *Miscellaneous History* (IV, 5).

18. See Sozomen, VI (37).

19. Ammianus Marcellinus, XXIX (XXXI, 4).

20. Among those who had received these orders, this one was involved in an infamous kind of love affair, that one was smitten with the beauty of a barbarian woman, and the rest were corrupted by such presents as linen clothing and blankets with fringes. They had no other care than filling their houses with slaves and their farms with livestock. Dexippus' *History.*

21. See Priscus' *History,* where this difference is shown clearly. It will perhaps be asked how nations that did not cultivate the soil could become so powerful, while those of America are so small. The reason is that pastoral peoples have a much

more secure subsistence than hunting peoples. It appears
from Ammianus Marcellinus that the Huns, in their original
abode, did not till the fields. They lived only on their flocks,
in a country abundant in pasture and watered by a number
of rivers, just as the natives of Little Tartary—inhabiting
a part of the same country—do today. It is likely that these
peoples began to cultivate the land after their departure,
when they inhabited places less suitable for raising flocks.

22. See Zosimus, IV (22-4). See also Dexippus, in Constantine
Porphyrogenitus' *Extract of Embassies.*

CHAPTER XVIII

NEW MAXIMS ADOPTED BY

THE ROMANS

Sometimes the cowardice of the emperors, often the weakness of the empire, brought about attempts to appease with money the peoples threatening invasion.[1] But peace cannot be bought, because the seller is then in a better position to compel it to be bought again.

It is preferable to run the risk of waging an unsuccessful war than to give money to assure peace. For a prince is always respected if it is known that it would take a long struggle to conquer him.

Besides, such gifts changed into tributes, and, freely given at the beginning, later became compulsory. They were considered acquired rights, and when an emperor refused them to some peoples, or wanted to give less, they became his mortal enemies. Among a thousand examples, the army Julian led against the Persians was pursued in its retreat by Arabs to whom he had refused the customary tribute.[2] And immediately afterward, under Valentinian's empire, the Alemanni, to whom smaller presents than usual had been offered, became indignant; and these peoples of the north, already swayed by the point of honor, avenged this pretended insult by a cruel war.

All these nations[3] surrounding the empire in Europe

and Asia absorbed the riches of the Romans little by little. And as the Romans had grown great because the gold and silver of all kings had been carried to them,[4] they grew weak because their gold and silver were carried to others.

The mistakes of statesmen are not always voluntary. Often they are the necessary consequences of the situation in which they find themselves, with difficulties giving rise to still more difficulties.

The military, as we have seen, had become very burdensome to the state. Soldiers received three kinds of benefits: their ordinary pay, some compensation once their service was over, and occasional gifts which quite often became rights for men who held the people and the prince in their hands.

The lack of funds to pay these expenses made it necessary to find a cheaper army. Treaties were made with barbarian nations, who had neither the luxury of the Roman soldiers, nor the same spirit, nor the same pretensions.

There was another advantage in this. Since barbarians fell on a country swiftly, needing no preparation once they resolved to move, it was difficult to levy troops in the provinces in time. The Romans therefore used for their defense another body of barbarians, always ready to receive money, to pillage, and to fight. They were served for the moment, but later there was as much trouble reducing their auxiliaries as their enemies.

The early Romans[5] did not put a greater number of auxiliary troops than Roman troops in their armies. And although their allies were really subjects, they did not want to have for subjects peoples who were more warlike than themselves.

In this later period, however, not only did they fail to observe this proportion of auxiliary troops, but they even filled the corps of national troops with barbarian soldiers.

Thus, they established practices wholly contrary to those that had made them universal masters. And, as formerly their constant policy was to keep the military art for themselves and deprive all their neighbors of it, they were now destroying it among themselves and establishing it among others.

Here, in a word, is the history of the Romans. By means of their maxims they conquered all peoples, but when they had succeeded in doing so, their republic could not endure. It was necessary to change the government, and contrary maxims employed by the new government made their greatness collapse.

It is not chance that rules the world. Ask the Romans, who had a continuous sequence of successes when they were guided by a certain plan, and an uninterrupted sequence of reverses when they followed another. There are general causes, moral and physical, which act in every monarchy, elevating it, maintaining it, or hurling it to the ground. All accidents are controlled by these causes. And if the chance of one battle—that is, a particular cause—has brought a state to ruin, some general cause made it necessary for that state to perish from a single battle. In a word, the main trend draws with it all particular accidents.

We see that the land forces of Denmark, for nearly two centuries, have almost always been beaten by those of Sweden. Apart from the courage of the two nations and the chances of war, there must be an inner vice [a] in the military or civil government of Denmark which has produced this effect—and I do not believe it is hard to discover.

Finally, the Romans lost their military discipline and went so far as to abandon their own arms. Vegetius says that when the soldiers found them too heavy, they obtained

---

[a] Truc, in his edition, suggests that Montesquieu may have been thinking of the defects of the Danish oligarchy and the weakened condition in which it kept the royal power prior to 1660. Jullian points to the internal struggle of the different orders as the main vice of the Danish government.

permission from the emperor Gratian to leave off the cuirass and then the helmet. And thus defencelessly exposed to the blows of the enemy, they no longer thought of anything but flight.[6]

He adds that they had lost the habit of fortifying their camp, and that, through this neglect, their armies were captured by the barbarian cavalry.

The cavalry of the early Romans was quite small. It comprised only an eleventh of each legion, very often less, and in view of the fact that we today have so many sieges to make, in which cavalry has little use, it is extraordinary that their cavalry was much smaller than ours. When the Romans were in decline, they had almost nothing but cavalry. It seems to me that the more expert a nation becomes in the military art, the more it makes use of infantry, and that the less it knows of that art, the more it enlarges its cavalry. The reason is that heavy or light infantry without discipline is worthless, whereas cavalry can always keep going, in its very disorder.[7] Cavalry's action consists more in its impetuosity and a certain shock, infantry's in its resistance and a certain immobility—it is rather a reaction than an action. In short, the force of cavalry is momentary, whereas infantry acts for a longer time; but this requires discipline.

The Romans succeeded in commanding all peoples not only by means of the art of war but also by their prudence, wisdom and constancy, and their love of glory and country. When all these virtues vanished under the emperors, the military art remained, and by it they kept what they had acquired in spite of the weakness and tyranny of their princes. But when corruption entered the military itself, the Romans became the prey of all peoples.

An empire founded by arms needs to be sustained by arms. But just as, when a state is in trouble, people cannot imagine how it can extricate itself, so, when a state is at peace and its power is respected, it does not occur to anyone how such a situation can change. Such a state therefore neglects its army, from which it believes it has nothing to hope for and everything to fear, and frequently even seeks to weaken it.

It was an inviolable rule of the early Romans that whoever had abandoned his post or lost his arms in battle was punished with death. Julian and Valentinian reestablished the old penalties in this respect. But the barbarians taken into Roman pay were accustomed to making war like the Tartars today—fleeing to fight again, seeking pillage rather than honor [8]—and were incapable of this kind of discipline.

Such was the discipline of the early Romans that generals had been known to condemn their sons to death for winning a victory without orders. But when they were mixed in with the barbarians, they contracted the spirit of independence which marked the character of these nations. And if you read of Belisarius' wars against the Goths, you will see a general whom his officers almost always disobeyed.

While the civil wars were raging, Sulla and Sertorius still preferred to perish rather than do anything from which Mithridates could profit. But in later times, as soon as a minister or some great man believed his avarice, vengeance or ambition would be served by letting the barbarians enter the empire, he immediately gave it over to their ravages. [9]

No states are in greater need of taxes than those which are growing weaker, so that burdens must be increased in proportion as the ability to pay decreases. Soon, in the Roman provinces, taxes became unbearable.

It is necessary to read, in Salvian, of the horrible exactions imposed on the population. [10] Pursued by tax farmers, the citizens could do nothing but seek refuge among the barbarians or surrender their liberty to the first person who wanted to take it.

This will explain, in our French history, the patience shown by the Gauls in enduring the revolution which was to estab-

lish so overwhelming a difference between a nation of nobles
and a nation of commoners. In making so many citizens
serfs—that is, slaves of the field to which they were attached
—the barbarians scarcely introduced anything which had not
been more cruelly practiced before them.[11]

NOTES

1. At first everything was given to the soldiers, later to the
   enemy.
2. Ammianus Marcellinus, XXV (6).
3. *Ibid.,* XXVI (5).
4. "You want riches?" said an emperor to his grumbling army.
   "There lies the country of the Persians; let us seek riches
   there. Believe me, nothing remains of the many treasures
   the Roman republic once possessed; and the evil stems from
   those who taught princes to buy the peace of the barbarians.
   Our finances are exhausted, our cities destroyed, our provinces ruined. An emperor who knows no other goods than
   those of the soul is not ashamed to confess an honest
   poverty." *Ibid.,* XXIV (3).
5. This is an observation made by Vegetius (III, 1); and it
   appears from Livy (XXI, 55) that if the number of
   auxiliaries sometimes exceeded, it was by very little.
6. *Military Matters,* I, 20.
7. Without observing any of our military maxims, the Tartar
   cavalry has done great things in all ages. See the *Narrations,*
   and especially those of the last conquest of China.
8. They had no desire to subject themselves to the labors of
   Roman soldiers. See Ammianus Marcellinus, XVIII (2),
   who mentions as an extraordinary thing that they did so on
   on occasion to please Julian, who wanted to put certain
   strongholds in a state of readiness.
9. This was not surprising in view of the intermixture that
   had taken place with nations which had been wandering,
   which knew no fatherland, and from which whole bodies of

troops often joined the victorious foe against their own nation. See, in Procopius (*The Gothic War*, I, 15) what the Goths were like under Vittigis.

10. See all of the fifth book of *The Government of God;* see also, in the *Embassy* written by Priscus, the talk of a Roman settled among the Huns about his happiness in that country.

11. Again see Salvian, V, and the laws of the *Code* (*Justinian,* XI, 47) and *Digest* (XXXIII, 7) on this point.

CHAPTER XIX

1. ATTILA'S GREATNESS

2. CAUSE OF THE SETTLEMENT

OF THE BARBARIANS

3. REASONS WHY THE WESTERN

EMPIRE WAS THE FIRST TO FALL

Since the Christian religion was established during the period of the empire's weakening, the Christians reproached the pagans for this decline, and the pagans held the Christian religion responsible. The Christians said that Diocletian had ruined the empire in taking on three colleagues,[1] because each emperor wanted to make as great outlays and maintain as strong armies as if he were alone. In this way, they claimed, the number of those receiving public funds bore no proportion to the number of those giving them, and tax burdens became so great that the lands were abandoned by their cultivators and turned into forests. The pagans, on the other hand, did not cease their outcry against the new religion, unheard of till then. And, as formerly in a flourishing Rome the floodings of the Tiber and the other effects of nature were attributed to the anger of the gods, so now, in dying Rome, misfortunes were imputed to the new religion and the overthrow of the old altars.

In a letter to the emperors concerning the altar of Victory,[a] a prefect named Symmachus made the most of the popular and hence most seductive objections to the Christian religion.

"What can better lead us to knowledge of the gods," he said, "than the experience of our past prosperity? We ought to be faithful to so many centuries, and follow our fathers who so successfully followed theirs. Imagine that Rome is talking to you, saying: Great princes, fathers of your country, respect my years, during which I have always observed the ceremonies of my ancestors. This religion has subjected the world to my laws; by it Hannibal was repulsed from my walls, and the Gauls from the Capitol. It is for the gods of our country that we ask peace; we ask it for the native gods. We do not enter into disputes fit only for idlers, and we wish to offer prayers, not blows." [2]

Three celebrated authors responded to Symmachus. Orosius composed his history to prove that there had always been as great evils in the world as those the pagans bemoaned. Salvian wrote a book maintaining that the disorders of the pagans had attracted the ravages of the barbarians.[3] And Saint Augustine showed that the city of heaven was different from this earthly city [4] in which the ancient Romans, for some human virtues, had received rewards that were as vain as these virtues.

We have said that in early times the policy of the Romans was to divide all the powers that offended them. Later they were unable to do so. They had to suffer Attila's sub-

---

[a] This altar stood in the hall where the senate met, and, starting with Constantine, became an object of contention between the Christian and pagan forces, the former desiring its removal, the latter its restoration. See Jullian.

jugating all the nations of the north. He extended his power
from the Danube to the Rhine, destroyed all the forts and
fortifications that had been erected on these rivers, and made
the two empires his tributaries.

"Theodosius," he had the insolence to say, "is, like
myself, the son of a very noble father. But in paying tribute
to me he is stripped of his nobility and has become my
slave. It is not just for him to lay snares for his master, like
a wicked slave."[5]

"It is not fitting," he said on another occasion, "for an
emperor to be a liar. He promised to give Saturnilus' daughter
in marriage to one of my subjects. If he does not wish to keep
his word, I declare war on him. If he cannot, and is so badly
off that his subjects dare to disobey him, I march to his
assistance."

We need not believe it was from moderation that Attila
let the Romans exist. He was following the ways of his nation,
which led him to subjugate peoples rather than conquer them.
This prince—in the wooden house in which Priscus portrays
him to us,[6] master of all barbarian nations and, in a way,
of almost all civilized ones[7]—was one of the great monarchs
of history.

At his court were seen the ambassadors of the Romans of
the East and West who came to receive his laws or implore
his mercy. Sometimes he demanded the return of fugitive
Huns or runaway Roman slaves; sometimes he wanted some
minister of the emperor handed over to him. He had placed
a tribute of twenty-one hundred pounds of gold on the empire
of the East. He received the salary of a general of the Roman
armies. He sent those he wanted to reward to Constantinople
to have them heaped with gifts, thus trafficking continually
on the fright of the Romans.

He was feared by his subjects, but it does not appear he
was hated by them.[8] Prodigiously proud, and yet wily; fierce
in his anger, but knowing how to pardon or defer punishment,

as it suited his interests; never making war when peace could give him sufficient advantage; faithfully served by the very kings who were his dependents—he had kept the Huns' old simplicity of manners for himself alone. Yet one can hardly praise for bravery the chief of a nation where children went into a frenzy at the recital of their fathers' splendid passages at arms, and fathers shed tears because they could not imitate their children.

After Attila's death, all the barbarian nations became divided again; but the Romans were so weak that there was no people so small it could not do them harm.

It was not a particular invasion that destroyed the empire, but all of them together. Since the invasion that was all but universal under Gallus, the empire seemed reestablished because it had not lost any territory. But it went by slow degrees from decline to fall, until it suddenly collapsed under Arcadius and Honorius.[b]

In vain were the barbarians driven back to their own country; they would have gone back anyhow to safeguard their booty. In vain were they exterminated; cities were sacked, villages burned, and families killed or dispersed nonetheless.[9]

When a province had been ravaged, the barbarians who followed found nothing left and had to pass on to another. At the beginning, they ravaged only Thrace, Moesia and Pannonia. When these countries were devastated, they destroyed Macedonia, Thessaly and Greece. From there they had to go to Noricum.[c] The empire—that is, the inhabited area—kept shrinking, and Italy became a frontier.

---

[b] Arcadius and Honorius: emperors of the East and West respectively (*c.* 400 A.D.).

[c] Moesia: a country to the south of the lower Danube; Noricum, Pannonia: areas north and northwest of the upper Adriatic Sea (Bavaria, Austria, Hungary).

The reason why no settlement of the barbarians occurred under Gallus and Gallienus was that they still found places to pillage.

Thus, when the Normans—who were just like the conquerors of the empire—had ravaged France for several centuries and found nothing left to take, they accepted a province which was entirely deserted and divided it among themselves.[10]

Since Scythia in those times was almost totally uncultivated,[11] its peoples were subject to frequent famines. They subsisted, in part, through commerce with the Romans that supplied them with provisions from provinces around the Danube.[12] In return the barbarians gave the things they had pillaged, the prisoners they had taken, and the gold and silver they received for peace. But when they could no longer pay these rather considerable tributes to keep themselves alive, they were forced to settle down.[13]

The Western empire was the first to fall. Here are the reasons why.

Having crossed the Danube, the barbarians found to their left the Bosporus, Constantinople, and all the forces of the Eastern empire stopping them. This made them turn to the right, towards Illyria, and push westward. A shifting of nations and a transporting of peoples away from that coast took place. Since the passages into Asia were better guarded, the whole movement flowed toward Europe, whereas in the first invasion, under Gallus, the forces of the barbarians split up.

Once the empire was really divided, the emperors of the East, who had alliances with the barbarians, did not want to break them for the sake of assisting the emperors of the West. This division of the administration, says Priscus,[14] was very prejudicial to the affairs of the West. Thus, because of their alliance with the Vandals, the Romans of the East [15] refused a fleet to those of the West. The Visigoths, having made an alliance with Arcadius, entered the West, and Honorius was forced to flee to Ravenna.[16] Finally, to get rid of Theodoric, Zeno [d] persuaded him to attack Italy, which Alaric had already ravaged.

There was a very close alliance between Attila and Genseric, king of the Vandals.[17] The latter feared the Goths.[18] He had married his son to the daughter of the king of the Goths; later, after having her nose cut off, he sent her back to her father; he therefore made common cause with Attila. The two empires, as if they were bound in chains by these two princes, did not dare help each other. The situation of the empire of the West was particularly deplorable. It had no sea power, all of which was in the East [19]—in Egypt, Cyprus, Phoenicia, Ionia, and Greece, the only countries where there was then some commerce. The Vandals and other peoples attacked all over the coasts of the West. A delegation of Italians came to Constantinople, says Priscus,[20] to report that affairs could not possible be kept going without a reconciliation with the Vandals.

Those who governed in the West were not impolitic. They judged it essential to save Italy, which was in one sense the head, in another the heart, of the empire. They made the barbarians pass to the outlying areas, and settled them there. The design was well conceived and well executed. These nations asked only for subsistence. They were given areas in the plains, but the mountainous regions, stream crossings, passes, and strongholds on the great rivers were kept from them, thus protecting Roman sovereignty. It is likely that these peoples would have been forced to become Romans; and the ease with which these destroyers were themselves destroyed by the Franks, the Greeks and the Moors is enough to substantiate this view. But this whole scheme was

---

[d] Zeno: Roman emperor of the East (474-91 A.D.).

upset by a revolution more fatal than all the others. The army of Italy, composed of foreigners, exacted what had been accorded to nations that were more foreign still. Under Odoacer, it formed an aristocracy that gave itself a third of the lands of Italy, thus delivering the mortal blow to this empire.

Amid so many misfortunes, one looked with sad curiosity for the fate of the city of Rome. It was, so to speak, defenseless. It could easily be starved; the extent of its walls made them very difficult to guard. Since it was situated on a plain, it could easily be taken by force; its people, extremely reduced in number, offered no resource. The emperors had to withdraw to Ravenna, a city formerly protected by the sea, like Venice today.

Almost always abandoned by their sovereigns, the Roman people began to become their own sovereign and make treaties for their preservation[21]—which is the most legitimate means of acquiring sovereign power. This is the way Amorica and Brittany began to live under their own laws.[22]

Such was the end of the Western empire. Rome had extended its power because its wars came only one at a time; by unbelievable good luck, each nation had attacked it only after the previous one had been ruined. Rome was destroyed because all nations attacked it at once and penetrated everywhere.

NOTES

1. Lactantius, *The Death of the Persecutors* (7).
2. Symmachus' *Letters,* X, letter 54.
3. *The Government of God.* (French editions other than Truc's refer to the "disorders of the Christians," not the pagans.)
4. *The City of God.*

---

[e] Amorica: the area bordering in the west coast of France.

5. *Gothic History* and *Narration of the Embassy* written by Priscus. It was Theodosius the younger.

6. Gothic History: *Hae sedes regis barbariem total tenentis, haec captis civitatibus habitacula praeponebat* (This was the abode of the king of the whole barbarian world, and he preferred it as a dwelling to the cities he captured).

7. It appears from Priscus' *Narration* that thought was being given at Attila's court to subduing even the Persians.

8. For the character of this prince and the manners of his court, it is necessary to consult Jordanes and Priscus.

9. The Goths were a very destructive nation. They had destroyed all the farmers in Thrace, and cut off the hands of all who drove wagons. Malchus' *Byzantine History*, in *The Extract of Embassies*.

10. In the chronicles gathered by André du Chesne, see the condition of this province toward the end of the ninth and the beginning of the tenth century. *Ancient Authors of Norman History*.

11. The Goths, as we have said, did not cultivate the soil. The Vandals called them *Trulles*, the name of a small measure, because in a famine they sold them such a measure of grain very dearly. Olympiodorus, in the *Library* of Photius, XXX.

12. From Priscus' *History* we see there were markets, established by treaty, along the banks of the Danube.

13. When the Goths sent a delegation to entreat Zeno to make Theodoric, the son of Triarius, his ally on the same terms he had accorded Theodoric, the son of Balamer, the senate was consulted. It answered that the revenues of the state were not sufficient to support two Gothic peoples, and that it was necessary to choose the friendship of one or the other. Malchus' *History*, in *The Extract of Embassies*.

14. Priscus, II.

15. *Ibid.*

16. Procopius, *War of the Vandals* (I, 2).

17. Priscus, II.

18. See Jordanes, *Gothic History*, 36.

19. This was especially apparent in the war between Constantine and Licinius.

20. Priscus, II.
21. During Honorius' reign, Alaric was besieging Rome and forced that city to make an alliance with him against the emperor himself, who could not oppose it. Procopius, *Gothic War,* I. See Zosimus, VI (6).
22. Zosimus, VI (5).

CHAPTER XX

1. JUSTINIAN'S CONQUESTS

2. HIS GOVERNMENT

Since all these peoples entered the empire pellmell, they got in each other's way. And policy at that time consisted entirely in arming them against each other—which, because of their ferocity and avarice, was easy. They destroyed each other for the most part before they were able to get settled, and this resulted in the eastern empire continuing for a time.

Moreover, the north exhausted itself, and those countless armies which appeared at first no longer emerged from it. After the early invasions of the Goths and the Huns, especially since the death of Attila, the Huns and the peoples following them attacked with less force.

When these nations which had gathered into a military body were dispersed as peoples, they weakened considerably. Spread out in the various places they conquered, they were themselves exposed to invasions.

It was in these circumstances that Justinian undertook to reconquer Africa and Italy, and did what our French carried out as successfully against the Visigoths, the Burgundians, the Lombards, and the Saracens.

When the Christian religion was brought to the barbarians, the Arian sect was practically dominant in the empire. Valens sent them Arian priests, who were their first apostles. But, in the interval between their conversion and their settlement, this sect was practically destroyed among the Romans. The Arian barbarians, finding the whole country orthodox, could never gain its good will, and it was easy for the emperors to disturb them.

Besides, these barbarians, whose art and genius hardly consisted in attacking cities, much less defending them, let their walls fall in ruins. Procopius informs us that Belisarius found the walls of Italy in this condition. Those of Africa had been pulled down by Genseric,[1] just as those of Spain later were by Vitisa,[2][a] with the intention of making sure of their inhabitants.

Upon settling in the countries of the south, most of these northern peoples at once adopted their indolence and became incapable of enduring the hardships of war.[3] The Vandals languished in sensual pleasure; dainties, effeminate clothes, baths, music, dancing, gardens, and theaters had become necessities to them.

They no longer worried the Romans,[4] says Malchus,[5] once they had stopped maintaining the armies that Genseric always held ready, and with which he forestalled his enemies, amazing everyone by the facility of his enterprises.

The Roman cavalry was well trained in drawing the bow, but that of the Goths and the Vandals used only the sword and lance, and could not fight at a distance.[6] To this difference Belisarius attributed part of his success.

The Romans, especially under Justinian, made good use of the Huns—peoples from whom the Parthians had come, and who fought like them. After losing their power through the defeat of Attila and the dissensions the large number of his children brought about, the Huns served the Romans as auxiliaries and formed their best cavalry.

All these barbarian nations were each distinguished by

---

[a] Vitisa: or Witiza, king of the Visigoths (c. 700 A.D.).

187 «   JUSTINIAN'S CONQUEST; HIS GOVERNMENT

their particular method of fighting and arming.[7] The Goths
and the Vandals were dangerous with the sword; the Huns
were admirable archers; the Suevi, good infantrymen; the
Alans were heavily armed, and the Herculi were a light troop.
The Romans took from all these nations the various bodies
of troops that suited their designs, and fought against any one
of them with the advantages of all the others.

Oddly enough, the weakest nations were the ones that
made the greatest settlements. We would be much deceived
if we judged their strength by their conquests. In this long
sequence of incursions, the barbarian peoples—or rather the
swarms emerging from them—either destroyed or were themselves destroyed. Everything depended on circumstances, and
while a great nation was fought or stopped, a troop of ad-
venturers who found a country unguarded made frightful
ravages there. The Goths, whose disadvantage in arms made
them flee before so many nations, settled in Italy, Gaul, and
Spain. The Vandals, leaving Spain because of their weakness, crossed over to Africa, where they founded a great
empire.

Justinian could equip only fifty vessels against the Vandals, and when Belisarius disembarked, he had only five
thousand soldiers.[8] It was a very bold enterprise. Leo, who
had formerly sent against them a fleet composed of all the
vessels of the East, carrying one hundred thousand men, had
not conquered Africa, and had come close to losing the
empire.

These great fleets, like great land armies, have hardly
ever succeeded. Since they exhaust a state, they can be neither
assisted nor repaired if the expedition is long or some misfortune strikes them. If a part is lost, what remains is useless
because the vessels of war and transport, the cavalry, the
infantry, the provisions—in short, the various parts—depend
on the whole. The slowness of the enterprise always results
in the enemy being found prepared. Besides, the expedition

rarely occurs at a favorable time; more likely, it will fall in a stormy season, since so many different things are seldom ready until several months after the time for which they were promised.

Belisarius invaded Africa, and it helped him considerably to draw a large quantity of provisions from Sicily by virtue of a treaty with Amalasuntha, queen of the Goths. When he was sent to attack Italy, he began by conquering Sicily, seeing that the Goths drew their subsistence from it. He starved his enemies, and found himself with an abundance of all things.

Belisarius took Carthage, Rome, and Ravenna, and sent the kings of the Goths and the Vandals as captives to Constantinople, where, after so long a time, the old triumphs were renewed.[9]

The main reasons for his successes can be found in the qualities of this great man.[10] With a general who followed all the maxims of the early Romans, an army much like the old Roman armies was formed.

In servitude the great virtues are usually hidden or lost; but the tyrannical government of Justinian could not crush the greatness of this soul or the superiority of this genius.

The eunuch Narses also served to make this reign illustrious. Because he was raised in the palace, the emperor had greater confidence in him, for princes always regard their courtiers as their most faithful subjects.

But Justinian's misconduct, his prodigality, harassment and plundering, his passion for building, changing and reforming, his inconstancy in his design, his severity and weakness in a reign made more disagreeable by a protracted old age—all these were real misfortunes, mixed with useless successes and fruitless glory.

These conquests, resulting from certain peculiar circumstances rather than from the strength of the empire, ruined everything. While the armies were occupied with them, new peoples crossed the Danube and desolated Illyria, Macedonia,

and Greece. And the Persians, in four invasions, inflicted in-
curable wounds on the East.[11]

The more rapid these conquests were, the less solidly were
they established; Italy and Africa were scarcely conquered
before it was necessary to reconquer them.

From the theater Justinian had taken a wife who had long
debased herself there.[12] The power she exerted over him was
unexampled in history, and by incessantly intruding the passions and fancies of her sex into public affairs, she corrupted
the greatest victories and successes.

In the East the number of wives has always been multiplied so as to remove the prodigious ascendancy they have
over us in those climates. But in Constantinople, the law re-
quiring a single wife gave dominion to this sex—which sometimes weakened the government.

The people of Constantinople had always been divided
into two factions: the *blues* and the *greens*. These originated
from a partiality formed in the theaters for some actors over
others. In circus games, the chariots whose drivers were
dressed in green vied with those dressed in blue, and everyone took an interest in them approaching frenzy.

These two factions were spread out in all the cities of
the empire, and the frenzy animating them grew in proportion
to the size of the cities—that is, to the idleness of a large part
of the people.

But the dissensions that are always necessary for maintaining republican government must be fatal to imperial rule,
their only effect being a change of sovereign rather than the
reestablishment of laws and the cessation of abuses.

Justinian, who favored the *blues* and refused all justice
to the *greens*,[13] embittered relations between the two factions
and consequently strengthened both.

They went so far as to destroy the authority of the magistrates. The *blues* did not fear the laws, because the emperor
protected them against the laws; the *greens* stopped respecting

the laws, because the laws could no longer protect them.[14]

All the bonds of friendship, kinship, duty, and gratitude were stripped away. Families destroyed themselves; every scoundrel who wanted to commit a crime belonged to the faction of the *blues,* and every man who was robbed or murdered belonged to the *greens.*

This government was even more cruel than it was unintelligent. Not content with doing a general injustice to his subjects by overwhelming them with excessive taxes, the emperor desolated them in their private affairs by all sorts of tyrannical acts.

I would not naturally be inclined to believe everything Procopius tells us on this subject in his *Secret History,* because the magnificent praises he has heaped on this prince in his other works weaken his testimony in this one, where he depicts him to us as the most stupid and cruel of tyrants.

But I confess that two things put me on the side of the *Secret History.* The first is that it fits in better with the amazing weakness of the empire at the end of this reign and in those following.

The other is a monument that still exists among us—the laws of this emperor—in which jurisprudence shows more changes in the course of a few years than it has in the last three hundred years of our monarchy.

These changes are mostly in things of such little importance [15] that one sees no reason why a legislator should have been induced to make them—unless one accepts the *Secret History*'s explanation charging Justinian with selling his judgments and his laws alike.

But what did the most harm to the political condition of the government was his scheme for reducing all men to the same opinion in matters of religion, in circumstances which made his zeal entirely indiscreet.

Just as the old Romans strengthened their empire by permitting every kind of religion in it, so was it subsequently reduced to nothing by amputating, one after the other, the sects which were not dominant.

These sects were entire nations. After being conquered by the Romans, some, like the Samaritans and Jews, had preserved their old religion. Others had spread out, like the sectarians of Montanus into Phrygia, or the Manicheans, Sabbatarians, and Arians into other provinces. Besides, a larger number of the rural population were still idolators obstinately attached to a religion as crude as themselves.

Justinian destroyed these sects by the sword and by his laws; forcing them to revolt, he was forced to exterminate them, with the result that many provinces were left uncultivated. He believed he had increased the number of the faithful; he had only diminished the number of men.

Procopius tells us that with the destruction of the Samaritans, Palestine became deserted. And what makes this a striking fact is that the empire was weakened by this zeal for religion in the very place where, some reigns later, the Arabs penetrated and destroyed it.

While the emperor carried intolerance to such lengths, it was exasperating that he himself did not agree with the empress on the most essential points. He followed the council of Chalcedonia, and the empress favored those who opposed it, whether—Evagrius tells us—they did so in good faith or for some ulterior motive.[16]

When we read Procopius on the buildings of Justinian, and see the strongholds and forts this prince erected everywhere, we constantly get the impression—the very false impression—of a flourishing state.

At first the Romans did not have any strongholds. They placed all their confidence in their armies, which they located along the rivers, building towers at certain intervals to lodge the soldiers.

But when they had nothing but weak armies, or often none at all, the frontier no longer defended the interior, and it was necessary to fortify it. And then they had more strongholds and less strength, more places of refuge and less security.[17] Since the countryside was no longer habitable except around fortified places, these were built on all sides. It was like France in the time of the Normans [18]—never so weak as when all its villages were surrounded by walls.

Thus all those lists of the names of forts Justinian built, with which Procopius covers entire pages, only testify to the empire's weakness.

NOTES

1. Procopius, *War of the Vandals,* I (5).
2. Mariana, *History of Spain,* VI, 19.
3. Procopius, *War of the Vandals,* II (6).
4. In the time of Hunneric.
5. *Byzantine History* in *The Extract of Embassies.*
6. See Procopius, *War of the Vandals,* I (8) and *War of the Goths.* The Gothic archers were on foot; they had little training.
7. A remarkable passage in Jordanes (L) tells us about all these differences. It occurs in connection with the battle the Gepidae fought against the sons of Attila.
8. Procopius, *War of the Goths,* II (24).
9. Justinian only accorded him a triumph for the conquest of Africa.
10. See the article *Belisarius* in Suidas.
11. The two empires ravaged each other all the more, since they had no hope of keeping what they had conquered.
12. The empress Theodora.
13. This malady was an old one. Suetonius says that Caligula, who was attached to the *greens,* hated the people for applauding the other faction.
14. For some idea of the spirit of those times, it is necessary to read Theophanes, who reports a long conversation that took place at the theater between the *greens* and the emperor.

15. See Justinian's *Novels*.
16. IV, 10.
17. Augustus had established nine frontiers or marches; under the succeeding emperors, their number increased. The barbarians showed up in places where they had not yet appeared, and Dio, LV, reports that in his time, under the empire of Alexander, there were thirteen of them. From the account of the state of the empire, written after the time of Arcadius and Honorius, we see there were fifteen in the eastern empire alone. Their number constantly increased. Pamphylia, Lycaonia, and Pisidia became marches, and the whole empire was covered with fortifications. Aurelian had been forced to fortify Rome.
18. And the English.

CHAPTER XXI

DISORDERS OF

THE EASTERN EMPIRE

In those times the Persians were in a more fortunate situation than the Romans. They had little fear of the peoples of the north,[1] because a part of Mount Taurus between the Caspian Sea and the Black Sea separated them from those peoples, and because they guarded a very narrow passage, closed by a gate,[2] that was the only place through which cavalry could pass. Everywhere else these barbarians had to descend precipices and leave their horses—on which their whole strength depended. But they were further impeded by the Araxes, a deep river flowing from west to east, the crossing places of which could easily be defended.[3]

Moreover, the Persians were undisturbed on their eastern frontier, while on the south they were bounded by the sea. It was easy for them to keep dissension alive among the Arab princes, whose only thought was to pillage one another. Hence they really had no enemies except the Romans. "We know," said an ambassador from Hormisdas,[4:a] "that the Romans are occupied with many wars, and have to fight against almost all nations. They know, on the other hand, that our only war is with them."

---

[a] This was Hormisdas IV, king of Persia (579-92 A.D.).

To the extent that the Romans had neglected the military art, the Persians had cultivated it. "The Persians," said Belisarius to his soldiers, "do not surpass you in courage; their only advantage over you is discipline."

In negotiations they acquired the same superiority as in war. On the pretext of having to keep a garrison at the Caspian Gates, they demanded a tribute from the Romans— as if every people did not have frontiers to guard. They exacted payment for peace, for truces, for armistices, for the time taken up with negotiations, and for the time they had spent making war.

When the Avars crossed the Danube, the Romans—who were usually occupied against the Persians when they should have been fighting the Avars, and against the Avars when they should have been stopping the Persians—were again forced to submit to a tribute; and the majesty of the empire was tarnished among all nations.

Justin, Tiberius and Maurice worked assiduously to defend the empire. Maurice had virtues, but they were sullied by an avarice unbelievable in a great prince.

The king of the Avars offered to return the prisoners he had taken to Maurice for half a piece of silver each; on his refusal, he had their throats cut. The indignant Roman army rebelled, and since the *greens* were in revolt at the same time, a centurion named Phocas was raised to the throne and had Maurice and his children put to death.

The history of the Greek empire—it is thus that we shall call the Roman empire henceforth—is nothing more than a tissue of revolts, seditions and perfidies. Subjects did not have the slightest idea of the loyalty owed to princes. And the succession of emperors was so interrupted that the title *porphyrogenitus*—that is, born in the rooms where the empresses gave birth—was a distinctive title few princes of the various imperial families could bear.

All paths could lead to imperial power. It was reached

by way of the soldiers, the clergy, the senate, the peasants, the people of Constantinople, and the people of other cities.

After the Christian religion became dominant in the empire, many heresies arose in succession that had to be condemned. When Arius denied the divinity of the Word, the Macedonians that of the Holy Spirit, Nestorius the unity of the person of Jesus Christ, Eutyches his two natures, and the monothelites his two wills, it was necessary to convene councils against them.ᵇ But since the decisions of these councils were not universally accepted at once, several emperors were seduced into returning to the condemned errors. And since no nation has ever had so violent a hatred of heretics as the Greeks, who believed themselves contaminated when they spoke to a heretic or lived with him, many emperors lost the affection of their subjects. And the peoples grew accustomed to thinking that princes—so often rebels against God—could not have been chosen by Providence to govern them.

Because of an opinion based on the idea that the blood of Christians must not be shed—an idea which established itself more and more once the Mohammedans had appeared —crimes not directly involving religion were punished lightly. Officials contented themselves with putting out the eyes, or cutting off the nose or hair, or in some way mutilating those who had incited some revolt or made an attempt on the person of the prince,⁵ so that such actions could be undertaken without danger, and even without courage.

Due to the respect people had for the imperial ornaments, anyone who dared put them on attracted immediate attention. It was a crime to wear purple materials or have them at home, but as soon as a man dressed in them he immediately gained a following, for respect attached more to the apparel than the person.

ᵇ These heresies ranged in time from the fourth to the seventh centuries A.D.

Ambition was further provoked by a strange mania of those times: there was hardly a man of repute who did not have in his possession some prediction promising him the empire.

Diseases of the mind are scarcely ever cured.[6] Judicial astrology[c] and the art of predicting by objects observed in a basin of water had replaced, for Christians, the divination by the entrails of sacrifices or the flight of birds that was abolished with paganism. Vain promises motivated most of the rash undertakings of individuals, just as they became the wisdom guiding the counsel of princes.

With the misfortunes of the empire growing every day, there was a natural inclination to attribute its failures in war and the shameful treaties it endured in times of peace to the misconduct of those who governed.

The revolutions that occurred themselves gave rise to other revolutions, and the effect in turn became the cause. Since the Greeks had seen so many different families come to the throne in succession, they were attached to none of them. And since chance had taken emperors from every walk of life, no birth was so low, or merit so slight, as to be able to extinguish hope.

Many precedents established in a nation form its general spirit, and create its manners, which rule as imperiously as its laws.

Great enterprises, it seems, are more difficult to conduct with us than they were with the ancients. They can hardly be concealed because communications among nations is such today that every prince has ministers in all courts, and can have traitors in all cabinets.

The invention of postal service makes news spread like lightning and arrive from all places.

---

[c] Judicial astrology studied the influence of the heavenly bodies on human destiny, while natural astrology made predictions of what we would now call astronomical phenomena.

Great enterprises cannot be accomplished without money, and merchants have been in control of money since the invention of letters of exchange. For this reason, the affairs of merchants are frequently bound up with the secrets of states, and these men neglect nothing to discover them.

Variations in the exchange rates, without a known cause, lead many people to look for the cause and at last to find it.

The invention of printing, which has put books in everyone's hands; the invention of engraving, which has made geographic maps so common; and, finally, the establishment of newspapers all make men better acquainted with matters of general interest, and this enables them to become informed of secret activities more easily.

Since the invention of postal service, conspiracies in the state have become more difficult because the public has all private secrets in its power.

Princes can act with dispatch because they have in their hands the forces of the state; conspirators must act slowly because they lack all resources. But now that everything is brought to light with more facility and dispatch, conspirators are discovered no matter how little time they lose in making their arrangements.

NOTES

1. The Huns.
2. The Caspian Gates.
3. Procopius, *War of the Persians,* I (10).
4. Menander's *Embassies.*
5. Zeno did much to bring about this slackening of punishments. See Malchus, *Byzantine History,* in *The Extract of Embassies.*
6. See Nicetas, *Life of Andronicus Comnenus* (II, 7).

CHAPTER XXII

WEAKNESS OF

THE EASTERN EMPIRE

In the confusion of things, when Phocas' hold on the throne was insecure, Heraclius came from Africa and had him killed. He found the provinces invaded and the legions destroyed.

Just after he had done something to remedy these evils, the Arabs sallied forth from their country to extend the religion and empire Mohammed had founded with the same hand.

Never was such rapid progress seen. In the first place, they conquered Syria, Palestine, Egypt, and Africa, and invaded Persia.

God did not permit His religion to lose its predominance in so many places because He had abandoned it, but because —whether its condition is one of outward humiliation or glory—it can always produce its natural effect, which is sanctification.

Religion and empires prosper in different ways. A celebrated author [a] said that he was quite content to be sick because sickness is a Christian's true condition. Similarly, one could say that the humiliations of the church, its dispersion,

---

[a] See Pascal's *Prière pour demander à Dieu le bon usage des maladies*, 11.

the destruction of its temples, the sufferings of its martyrs are the occasions of its glory, and that when in the eyes of the world it appears to be triumphant, the time of its degradation is usually at hand.

To explain this famous event involving the conquest of so many countries by the Arabs, one need not have recourse to enthusiasm alone. The Saracens had for a long time been distinguished among the auxiliaries of the Romans and Persians; the Osroenians [b] and they were the best archers in the world. Alexander Severus and Maximin had engaged them in their service as much as possible, and had used them with great success against the Germans, whom they devastated from afar. Under Valens the Goths could not resist them.[1] In short, they were the best cavalry in the world at that time.

We have said that with the Romans the legions of Europe were better than those of Asia. The opposite held true of their cavalry; I refer to the cavalry of the Parthians, Osroenians and Saracens. And what stopped the conquests of the Romans was that, after the time of Antiochus, a new Tartar people whose cavalry was the best in the world seized upper Asia.

This cavalry was heavy,[2] while Europe's was light; today it is the opposite. Holland and Friesland were not yet made,[3] so to speak, and Germany was full of woods, lakes and marshes, where cavalry was of little use.

After the rivers were changed in their course, these marshes disappeared, and the appearance of Germany altered. The works of Valentinian on the Neckar, and those of the Romans on the Rhine,[4] brought about many transformations.[5] And, with the establishment of commerce, regions which previously did not produce horses did so. and they were put to use.[6]

After Constantine, the son of Heraclius, had been poisoned and his son, Constans, killed in Sicily, Constantine the

---

[b] Osroenians: a people in northwestern Mesopotamia.

Bearded, his eldest son, succeeded him.[7] The notables of the provinces of the East assembled and wanted to crown his two other brothers, maintaining that just as it was necessary to believe in the Trinity, so it was reasonable to have three emperors.

Greek history is full of such features. Once small-mindedness succeeded in forming the nation's character, wisdom took leave of its enterprises, and disorders without cause, as well as revolutions without motive, appeared.

A universal bigotry numbed the spirit and enervated the whole empire. Properly speaking, Constantinople is the only Eastern land where the Christian religion has been dominant. Now the faintheartedness, laziness, and indolence of the nations of Asia blended into religious devotion itself. Among a thousand examples, I need only mention that of Philippicus, Maurice's general, who, on the point of giving battle, began to cry at the thought of the great number of men who were going to be killed.[8]

The tears certain Arabs shed in grief, when their general made a truce which prevented them from spilling the blood of Christians, were another thing entirely.[9]

For a fanatic army and a bigoted army are totally different. We see this in a famous revolution of modern times, when Cromwell's army was like the Arabs', and the armies of Ireland and Scotland like the Greeks'.

A crude superstition, which degrades the mind as much as religion elevates it, made all virtue consist in an ignorant and stupid passion for icons, and caused men to place their entire confidence in them. And generals were known to lift a siege [10] and lose a city [11] in order to get a relic.

The Christian religion degenerated under the Greek empire to the point it had reached in our day among the Moscovites, before Czar Peter I regenerated the nation and introduced more changes in the state he governed than conquerors introduce in those they usurp.

It is easy to believe that the Greeks fell into a kind of idolatry. The Italians and Germans of those times cannot be suspected of having been little attached to the externals of worship. However, when the Greek historians refer to the scorn of the Italians for relics and icons, it sounds like the declamations of our controversialists against Calvin. When the Germans passed through on their way to the Holy Land, Nicetas says the Armenians received them as friends because they did not worship icons. Now if, in the view of the Greeks, the Italians and Germans did not have enough such worship, what must have been the enormity of their own?

The East was on the point of witnessing much the same revolution that occurred about two centuries ago in the West, when, with the revival of letters, people began to sense the abuses and irregularities into which they had fallen. And while everyone was seeking a remedy for these evils, men who were bold but insufficiently docile shattered the Church instead of reforming it.

Leo the Isaurian, Constantine Copronymus, and Leo, his son, made war against the icons. And after the empress Irene had reestablished their worship, Leo the Armenian, Michael the Stammerer and Theophilus [c] abolished them again. These princes believed they could moderate this worship only by destroying it. They made war on the monks who disturbed the state,[12] and, always using extreme methods, wanted to exterminate them by the sword instead of seeking to regulate them.

Accused of idolatry by the partisans of the new opinions, the monks [13] threw them off the track by accusing them, in turn, of magic.[14] And showing the people the churches denuded of icons and of all that had previously constituted the object of their veneration, they did not let them imagine that

---

[c] Irene, Leo, etc.: rulers in the eighth and ninth centuries A.D.

such churches could serve any purpose other than sacrificing to devils.

The quarrel about icons was so intense that it eventually became impossible for sensible men to propose a moderate solution, and this was because of its bearing on a very delicate issue—namely, power. For having usurped power, the monks could not increase or maintain it without constantly adding to the externals of worship, of which they themselves formed a part. That is why the wars against icons were always wars against them, and why, when they had won their point, their power knew no bounds.

The same thing then happened that happened again a few centuries later [d] in the quarrel Barlaam and Acindynus had with the monks, which tormented the empire until its destruction. A dispute arose as to whether the light that appeared around Christ on Mount Tabor was created or uncreated. The monks could not really care less whether it was one or the other, but since Barlaam was directly attacking them, the light had of necessity to be uncreated.

Because of the war the iconoclastic emperors declared on the monks, the principles of the government were revitalized a little, public revenues were used for the public, and, finally, the fetters were removed from the body of the state.

When I think of the profound ignorance into which the Greek clergy plunged the laity, I cannot keep from making comparisons with those Scythians in Herodotus [15] who put out the eyes of their slaves so that distractions would not keep them from churning milk.

The empress Theodora brought the icons back, and the monks began to abuse public piety again. They went so far as to oppress the secular clergy itself, occupying all the great sees, [16] and gradually excluding all ecclesiastics from the epis-

---

[d] This took place in the fourteenth century.

copacy. That is what made these monks intolerable. If we compare them with the Latin clergy and also compare the conduct of the popes with that of the patriarchs of Constantinople, we see men who were as wise as the others were unintelligent.

Here now is a strange inconsistency of the human mind. The ministers of religion among the early Romans were not excluded from the burdens of evil society and hardly got involved in its affairs. When the Christian religion was established, the ecclesiastics, who were more removed from worldly affairs, concerned themselves with them to a moderate extent. But when, in the decline of the empire, the monks were the only clergy, these men—destined by more particular vows to flee and fear worldly affairs—seized every occasion to take part in them. They never stopped making a stir everywhere and agitating the world they had quitted.

No affairs of state, no peace, no war, no truce, no negotiation, no marriage was arranged except through the monks. The prince's councils were full of them, and the nation's assemblies almost wholly composed of them.

The evil this caused would pass belief. They enfeebled the mind of princes, and made them do even good things imprudently. While Basil employed the warriors of his navy in building a church to Saint Michael, he let the Saracens pillage Sicily and take Syracuse. And Leo, his successor, who employed his fleet for the same purpose, let them occupy Tauromenium [e] and the island of Lemnos.[17]

Andronicus Palaeologus abandoned his navy on being assured that God was so happy with his zeal for the peace of the Church that his enemies would not dare attack him. The same prince feared that God would demand an account of the time he spent governing his state—time stolen from spiritual affairs.[18]

---

[e] Tauromenium: a town in Sicily.

Great talkers, great disputants and natural sophists that they were, the Greeks never stopped embroiling religion in controversies. Since the monks had great prestige at the court, which was even weaker as it grew more corrupt, the monks and the court had the effect of corrupting each other, and the evil was in them both. The result was that the entire attention of the emperors was occupied, sometimes in calming, often in irritating, theological disputes—which have always been observed to become more frivolous as they become more heated.

On seeing the frightful ravages of the Turks in Asia, Michael Palaeologus, whose reign was in such agitation over religious disputes, exclaimed, with a sigh, that the rash zeal of certain persons who had decried his conduct and raised his subjects in revolt against him had forced him to apply all his cares to his own preservation and to neglect the ruin of the provinces. "I rested satisfied," he said, "with providing for these distant parts through governors, who—either because they were won over by money or feared being punished—have concealed the needs of these areas from me." [19]

The patriarchs of Constantinople had immense power. During popular tumults the emperors and notables of the state withdrew to the churches, and since the patriarch made the decision to hand them over or not, and exercised this right as he fancied, he proved always, though indirectly, to be the arbiter of all public affairs.

When Andronicus the elder [20] made known to the patriarch that he should concern himself with the affairs of the Church and let him govern the empire, the patriarch replied: "It is as if the body said to the soul: I claim to have nothing in common with you, and I have no need at all of your help in performing my functions."

Since such monstrous pretensions were insufferable to the princes, the patriarchs were often driven from their sees. But in a superstitious nation—where all the ecclesiastical activities of a patriarch thought to be a usurper were held in abomination—this brought about continual schisms, with each patriarch—the old, the new, the newest—having his own votaries.

Quarrels of this sort were far more grievous than those over dogma, because they were like a hydra that a new deposition could always regenerate.

Raging disputes became so natural a condition to the Greeks that when Cantacuzene took Constantinople he found the emperor John and the empress Ann preoccupied with a council against some enemies of the monks.[21] And when Mohammed I besieged the city, he could not suspend the theological hatreds [22] there, and people were more preoccupied with the council of Florence than with the Turkish army.[23;f]

In ordinary disputes each person knows he can be wrong and hence is not extremely opinionated or obstinate. But in our disputes over religion, by the nature of the thing, each person is sure his opinion is true, and we are indignant with those who obstinately insist on making us change instead of changing themselves.

Readers of Pachymeres' history will easily perceive the inability of theologians, then and always, ever to come to an agreement by themselves. In its pages we see an emperor [24] who spends his life calling them together, listening to them, reconciling them, and yet we also see a hydra of disputes that constantly keep arising. And we feel that with the same method, the same patience, the same hopes, the same desire to reach a conclusion, the same simple attitude towards their intrigues, the same respect for their hatreds, they would

---

f The union of the Greek and Latin churches, decided upon at the council of Florence (1439 A.D.), was celebrated at Saint Sophia (The Great Church).

never have come to an agreement to the very end of the world.

Here is quite a remarkable example. At the emperor's urging, the partisans of the patriarch Arsenius made an agreement with those of the patriarch Joseph, stipulating that each of the two parties would write its claims on a separate paper; that the two papers would be thrown into a fire; that if one of the two remained whole the judgment of God would be obeyed; and that if both were consumed, they would renounce their differences. The fire destroyed both papers; the two parties united, and for a day there was peace. But the next day they said that the change in their views should have depended on an inner persuasion and not on chance, and the war was resumed more intensely than ever.[25]

One should pay great attention to the disputes of theologians, but as covertly as possible. The trouble one seems to take in pacifying them adds to their prestige; it shows that their thinking is so important that it determines the tranquillity of the state and the security of the prince.

One can no more put an end to their involvements by listening to their subtleties than one could abolish duels by establishing schools for refining upon the point of honor.

The Greek emperors had so little prudence that, when the disputes lay dormant, they were insane enough to revive them. Anastasius,[26] Justinian,[27] Heraclius,[28] and Manuel Comnenus[29] proposed points of faith to their clergy and people, who would have rejected the truth in their mouths even if they found it there. Thus, always offending in form, and usually in matter, and desirous of displaying a penetration they could well have shown in so many of the other affairs entrusted to them, they undertook vain disputes on the nature of God. But the God who conceals Himself from the learned because of their pride does not reveal himself any the more to the powerful.

It is an error to believe that any human authority exists in the world which is despotic in all respects. There never has been one, and never will be, for the most immense power is always confined in some way. Let the Grand Seignior [g] impose a new tax on Constantinople, and a general outcry immediately makes him aware of limits he had not known. A king of Persia can easily compel a son to kill his father, or a father to kill his son;[30] but as for making his subjects drink wine, he cannot do it. There exists in each nation a general spirit on which power itself is based, and when it shocks this spirit it strikes against itself and necessarily comes to a standstill.

The most vicious source of all the misfortunes of the Greeks is that they never knew the nature or limits of ecclesiastical and secular power, and this made them fall, on both sides, into continual aberrations.

This great distinction, which is the basis on which the tranquillity of peoples rests, is founded not only on religion but also on reason and nature, which ordain that really separate things—things that can endure only by being separate— should never be confounded.

Although, with the ancient Romans, the clergy did not constitute a separate body, this distinction was as well known to them as to us. Clodius had consecrated Cicero's house to Liberty,[h] and when Cicero returned from exile he demanded it back. The pontiffs decided that it could be returned to him without offending against religion if it had been consecrated without an express order of the people. "They declared, "Cicero tells us,[31;i] "that they had examined only

---

[g] Grand Seignior: a title formerly given to the Sultan of Turkey.

[h] Exiling Cicero and seizing his house was part of Clodius' effort to destroy him.

[i] At this point some French editors include in the footnote the Latin quotation from Cicero.

the validity of the consecration, and not the law made by the people; that they had judged the first item as pontiffs, and would judge the second as senators."

NOTES

1. Zosimus, IV (22).
2. See what Zosmius says in I (50) about the cavalry of Aurelian and that of Palmyra. See also Ammianus Marcellinus (XXIV, 6) on the cavalry of the Persians.
3. These were, for the most part, submerged lands artificially made suitable for human habitation.
4. See Ammianus Marcellinus, XXVII (XXVIII, 2).
5. The climate is no longer as cold there as the ancients said it was.
6. Caesar says the horses of the Germans were ungainly and small, IV, 2. And Tacitus, in *The Manners of the Germans* (5), says: *Germania pecorum fecunda, sed pleraque improcera* (Germany is rich in flocks and herds, but most are small in size).
7. Zonaras, *Life of Constantine the Bearded.*
8. Theophylactus, II, 3, *History of the Emperor Maurice.*
9. *History of the Conquest of Syria, Persia and Egypt by the Saracens,* by Ockley.
10. Zonaras, Life of *Romanus Lecapenus.*
11. Nicetas, *Life of John Comnenus.*
12. Long before, Valens had made a law to force them to go to war, and he had all those who disobeyed put to death. Jordanes, *The Succession of Reigns;* and law 26 of *De Decursionibus,* in the Code Justinian (X, title 32).
13. Nothing the reader finds here about the Greek monks reflects on their order itself, for we cannot say a thing is not good just because it has been abused in certain times and places.
14. Leo the Grammarian, *Life of Leo the Armenian,* and *Life of Theophilus.* See Suidas for the article on *Constantine,* son of Leo.

15. IV (2).
16. See Pachymeres, VIII (28).
17. Zonaras and Nicephorus, *Lives of Basil and Leo.*
18. Pachymeres, VII (26).
19. Pachymeres, VI, 29. President Cousin's translation has been used.
20. Paleologus. See the *History of the Two Andronici,* written by Cantacuzene, I, 50.
21. Cantacuzene, III, 99.
22. Ducas, *History of the Last Paleologi* (37).
23. *Ibid.* They were wondering whether they had heard mass from a priest who had consented to the union; they would have avoided him as they would a conflagration, and considered the great church a profane temple. The monk Gennadius flung his anathemas at all those desiring peace.
24. Andronic Paleologus.
25. Pachymeres, I.
26. Evagrius, III (30).
27. Procopius, *Secret History* (XI, XIII).
28. Zonaras, *Life of Heraclius* (XIV, 17).
29. Nicetas, *Life of Manuel Comnenus* (VII, 5).
30. See Chardin (*Description of the Political, Civil and Military Government of the Persians,* 2).
31. *Letters to Atticus,* IV (letter 2).

CHAPTER XXIII

1. REASON FOR THE DURATION

OF THE EASTERN EMPIRE

2. ITS DESTRUCTION

After what I have just said about the Greek empire, it is natural to ask how it was able to last so long. I believe I can give the reasons.

After the Arabs had attacked it and conquered some of its provinces, their leaders disputed over the caliphate. And the fire of their early zeal no longer produced anything but civil discords.

After the same Arabs conquered Persia and became divided or weakened there, the Greeks no longer had to keep the principal forces of their empire on the Euphrates.

An architect named Callinicus, who came to Constantinople from Syria, had discovered the composition of a fire that was blown forth from a tube and was such that water and whatever else extinguishes ordinary fires only intensified the blaze. For centuries the Greeks, who made use of it, were in a position to burn all the fleets of their enemies, especially those of the Arabs, who came from Africa or Syria to attack them at Constantinople.

This fire was classified as a state secret. And Constantine Porphyrogenitus, in his book on the administration of the empire dedicated to his son, Romanus, warns him against giving it away. He tells him that when the barbarians ask for the *Greek fire* he should reply that he is not permitted to give it to them because an angel, who brought it to the emperor Constantine, forbade its transfer to other nations, and that those who had dared to do so had been consumed by the fire of heaven upon entering a church.

Constantinople carried on the greatest and almost the only commerce in the world, at a time when the Gothic nations on one side, and the Arabs on the other, had ruined commerce and industry everywhere else. The making of silk had come over from Persia, and, since the invasion of the Arabs, was badly neglected in Persia itself; besides, the Greeks had control of the sea. This brought immense riches into the state, and consequently, great resources; and as soon as it experienced some respite, public prosperity reappeared at once.

Here is a notable example. Andronicus Comnenus the elder was the Nero of the Greeks, but, with all his vices, he showed an admirable firmness in preventing the injustices and harassments of the great; and it was observed that [1] several provinces again grew strong during the three years he reigned.

Finally, since the barbarians who lived along the banks of the Danube had settled down, they were no longer so frightening and even served as a barrier against other barbarians.

Thus, while the empire was weighed down by a bad government, particular causes supported it. So today we see some European nations maintaining themselves, in spite of their weakness, by the treasuries of the Indies; we see the temporal states of the pope maintaining themselves by the respect in which their sovereign is held, and the corsairs of Barbary by the impediments they present to the commerce of the small nations, which makes them useful to the great ones. [2]

The Turkish empire is currently about as weak as was

the Greek empire formerly. But it will last a long time, for if any prince whatsoever endangered it in pursuing his conquests, the three commercial powers of Europe know their own interests too well not to go to its defense immediately.[3]

It is a good thing for them that God has allowed the existence of nations suited for needlessly possessing a great empire.

In the time of Basil Porphyrogenitus, the power of the Arabs was destroyed in Persia. Mohammed, the son of Sambrael, who reigned there, called three thousand Turks from the north to serve as auxiliaries.[4] Because of some disaffection, he sent an army against them, but they put it to flight. Indignant with his soldiers, Mohammed ordered them to pass before him dressed in the frocks of women, but they joined the Turks, who at once proceeded to remove the garrison guarding the bridge over the Araxes and opened the crossing to an innumerable multitude of their compatriots.

After conquering Persia, they spread from east to west over the territories of the empire. And when Romanus Diogenes wanted to stop them, they took him prisoner and subjugated almost everything the Greeks possessed in Asia up to the Bosporus.

Some time afterwards, in the reign of Alexius Comnenus, the Latins attacked the East. Long before, an unfortunate schism [a] had filled the nations of the two rites with an implacable hatred for each other, and it would have blazed forth sooner if the Italians had stopped thinking of repressing the emperors of Germany, whom they feared, rather than the Greek emperors, whom they merely hated.

It was in these circumstances that a new religious opinion

---

[a] Alexius Comnenus reigned from 1081 to 1118 A.D. The estrangement between the eastern and Roman parts of Christianity had been growing for several centuries, with the formal break occurring in 1054 A.D.

suddenly spread through Europe, to the effect that—since the infidels were profaning the places where Jesus Christ was born or had suffered—a man could efface his sins by taking up arms to drive them out. Europe was full of men who loved war, and who had many crimes to expiate, which it was proposed that they do by following their ruling passion. Everyone therefore took up the cross and arms.

Arriving in the East, the crusaders besieged Nicaea and captured it. They returned it to the Greeks; and, to the consternation of the infidels, Alexius and John Comnenus drove the Turks back to the Euphrates again.

But whatever the advantage the Greeks could gain from the crusaders' expeditions, there was no emperor who failed to shudder at the peril of seeing such proud heroes and great armies pass in succession through the heart of his states.

They sought therefore to make Europe lose its taste for these undertakings, and the crusaders met everywhere with betrayals, perfidy, and all that can be expected from a timorous enemy.

We must admit that the French, who had begun these expeditions, did nothing to make themselves bearable. From the invectives of Andronicus Comnenus [b] against us,[5] we really see that while we were in a foreign nation we failed to restrain ourselves, and that even then we had the defects for which we are reproached today.

A French count was going to seat himself on the emperor's throne. Count Baldwin took him by the arm and said: "You should know that when you are in a country you must follow its customs." "Indeed," he answered, "what a boor this fellow is to sit down here while so many captains are standing!"

---

[b] Jullian points out that the text should read Anna Comnena (instead of Andronicus Comnenus), as it did originally in 1734. Anna was Alexius' daughter.

The Germans, who passed through afterward, and were the nicest sort of people, paid a heavy penalty for our blunders, and everywhere found people in whom we had aroused feelings of revulsion.

Finally, hatred reached fever pitch, and the French and Venetians, led by some bad treatment given Venetian merchants and by ambition, avarice and a false zeal, decided to crusade against the Greeks.

They found them as little inured to war as, in recent times, the Tartars found the Chinese. The French made fun of their effeminate attire, walked the streets of Constantinople dressed in their garish robes, and carried pen and paper in their hands to mock this nation which had renounced the profession of arms.[7] And after the war they refused to admit any Greek whatsoever into their troops.

They captured the entire western part of the empire, and elected as emperor the Count of Flanders, the remoteness of whose states could not give the Italians any grounds for jealousy. The Greeks maintained themselves in the East, separated from the Turks by the mountains and from the Latins by the sea.

Since the Latins, who had met with no obstacles in pursuing their conquests, met with an infinite number in securing them, the Greeks crossed back from Asia to Europe, retaking Constantinople and nearly the whole West.

But this new empire was only a shadow of the former, and had neither its resources nor its power.

In Asia almost its sole possessions were the provinces west of the Meinder and Sakaria,[c] and most of the provinces in Europe were divided into petty sovereignties.

Moreover, during the sixty years that Constantinople remained in the hands of the Latins—with the vanquished

---

[c] Meinder and Sakaria: rivers in western Asia Minor.

dispersed and the victors occupied with war—commerce passed entirely into the control of the Italian cities, and Constantinople was deprived of its riches.

Even its internal commerce was carried on by the Latins. The Greeks, having just reestablished their rule, wished to conciliate the Genoese by according them the freedom to trade without paying duties.[8] And the Venetians, who did not accept a peace but only some truces, and whom the Greeks did not want to irritate, did not pay duties either.

Before the capture of Constantinople, Manuel Comnenus had permitted the navy to decay, but since commerce still existed it could easily be strengthened again. When the navy was abandoned in the new empire, however, the evil was without remedy because the lack of power constantly increased.

This state, which ruled over many islands, which was divided by the sea and surrounded by it in so many places, had no vessels to navigate it. The provinces no longer had any communication with each other. Their inhabitants were forced to take refuge further inland to avoid pirates, and after doing so they were ordered to withdraw into fortresses to save themselves from the Turks.[9]

The Turks were then waging a peculiar war against the Greeks. They were literally on a manhunt, and sometimes crossed two hundred leagues of country to commit their ravages. Since they were divided under several sultans, one could not, by means of presents, make peace with all, and it was useless to make it with some.[10] They had turned Mohammedan, and zeal for their religion gave them a marvelous commitment to ravaging the lands of Christians. Besides, since they were the ugliest peoples on earth, their women were frightful like themselves,[11] and as soon as they had seen Greek women they could no longer bear any others.[12] This led them to continual abductions. Finally, they had at all times been given to brigandage; and it was these same Huns who had formerly brought so much evil upon the Roman empire.

With the Turks inundating all that remained of the Greek empire in Asia, the inhabitants who could escape fled before them to the Bosporus. And those who found vessels took refuge in the European part of the empire, which considerably increased the number of its inhabitants. But this number soon diminished. Such raging civil wars broke out that the two factions called in various Turkish sultans on the condition [13] —as extravagant as it was barbarous—that all the inhabitants captured in the regions of the opposing party would be led into slavery. And with a view to ruining their enemies, both concurred in destroying the nation.

After Bajazet [d] had subdued all the other sultans, the Turks would have done what they have since done under Mohammed II, had they not themselves been on the point of being exterminated by the Tartars.

I do not have the courage to speak of the calamities which followed. I will only say that, under the last emperors, the empire—reduced to the suburbs of Constantinople—ended like the Rhine, which is no more than a brook when it loses itself in the ocean.

NOTES

1. Nicetas, *Life of Andronicus Comnenus,* II.
2. They disturbed the Italians' navigation in the Mediterranean.
3. Thus the plans against the Turks, such as the one formed under Leo X's pontificate, according to which the emperor was to go to Constantinople through Bosnia, and the king of France through Albania and Greece, while other princes were to embark from their own ports. These plans, I say,

---

[d] Bajazet reigned from 1389 to 1402 A.D.

were not serious, or were undertaken by people who did not see what was in Europe's interest.

4. History written by Nicephorus-Bryennius Caesar, *Lives of Constantine Ducas and Romanus Diogenes.*

5. *History of Alexius,* her father, X, XI.

6. Nicetas, *History of Manuel Comnenus,* I.

7. Nicetas, *History,* After the Capture of Constantinople, 3.

8. Cantacuzene, IV (25).

9. Pachymeres, VII (37).

10. Cantacuzene, III, 96, and Pachymeres, XI, 9.

11. This gave rise to the tradition of the north, related by the Goth Jordanes (XXIV), that Philimer, king of the Goths, found some sorceresses upon entering Getic territory and drove them far from his army. They wandered in the wilderness, where nightmarish demons mated with them, thus spawning the nation of the Huns. *Genus ferocissimum, quod fuit primum inter paludes, minutum, tetrum atque exile, nec alia voce notum, nisi quae humani sermonis imaginem assignabat* (a most savage race, which first lived in the marshes, small, ugly, and skinny, and marked by no other utterance than one which gave them a semblance of human speech).

12. Michael Ducas, *History of John Manuel, John and Constantine,* 9. At the beginning of his *Extract of Embassies,* Constantine Porphyrogenitus warns that when the barbarians come to Constantinople, the Romans should keep from showing them the greatness of their wealth and the beauty of their women.

13. See note 11 above.

14. See the *History of the Emperors John Paleologus and John Cantacuzene,* written by Cantacuzene (III, 81, 96).

INDEX

A

—— in general, they make a people more warlike and more dangerous to its neighbors, 107
—— two kinds in France, 121
Claudius (the emperor) gives his officers the right to administer justice, 138
Clemency (whether the) of a successful usurper deserves great praise, 108
Cleopatra flees at the battle of Actium, 120
—— undoubtedly intended winning Octavius' heart, 120
Colonies, Roman, 46
Comitia, became tumultuous, 93
Commerce: reasons why the power it brings to a nation is not always of long duration, 47
—— and arts were considered servile occupations among the Romans, 98-99
Commodus succeeds Marcus Aurelius, 146
Comnenus (Andronicus): see Andronicus.
—— Alexis: see Alexis
—— John: see John
—— Manuel: see Manuel
Compass (the invention of) has led to a great development of navigation, 48
Conquests of the Romans, slow at the beginning, but continual, 28
—— more difficult to keep than to make, 52
Conspiracies frequent at the beginning of Augustus' reign, 110
—— more difficult than they were among the ancients: why, 199
Conspiracy against Caesar, 109-110
Constans, grandson of Heraclius through Constantine, killed in Sicily, 202
Constantine transfers the seat of the empire to the East, 159
—— distributes grain at Constantinople and Rome, 159
—— withdraws the Roman legions, stationed along the frontiers, to the interior of the provinces: results of this innovation, 161
Constantine, son of Heraclius, poisoned, 202
Constantine the Bearded, son of Constans, succeeds his father, 202-203
Constantipole: named after Constantine, 159
—— divided into two factions, 189
—— immense power of its patriarchs, 207
—— is maintained by its commerce under the last Greek emperors, 214
—— captured by the Crusaders, 217
—— taken back by the Greeeks, 217
—— its commerce ruined, 218
Constantius sends Julian to Gaul, 161
Consuls, annual; their establishment at Rome, 26
Coriolanus: the senate's tone in treating with him, 50
Country (the love of) was a kind of religious sentiment among the Romans, 98
Courage, martial: its definition, 36
Crusaders, make war on the Greeks and crown the count of Flanders emperor, 217
—— hold Constantinople for sixty years, 217
Crusades, 216 ff.
Cynoscephale (battle of), where Philip was vanquished by the Aetolians in combination with the Romans, 59

D

E

East (condition of the) at the time of the Carthaginians' total defeat, 60 ff.
—— this empire outlasts that of the West: why, 179
—— Justinian's conquests only hasten its ruin, 188-189
—— why, in all ages, the plurality of wives has been practiced there, 189
—— why it lasted so long beyond that of the West, 213 ff.
—— what upheld it despite the weakness of its government, 214
—— total collapse of this empire, 219
Egypt: sketch of this kingdom's government after Alexander's death, 60-61
—— misconduct of its kings, 63
—— the composition of their principal forces, 64
—— the Romans deprive them of auxiliary troops drawn from Greece, 64
—— conquered by Augustus, 160
Emperors, Roman, were, as such, commanders of the armies, 123
—— their power grows by degrees, 129
—— the cruelest ones were not in the least hated by the common people: why, 137
—— were proclaimed by the Roman armies, 139
—— inconvenience of this form of election, 139
—— try in vain to gain respect for the senate's authority, 139-140
—— Nero's successors, up to Vespasian, 140
—— their power could appear more tyrannical than that of present-day princes: why, 146-147
—— often foreigners: why, 148
—— murders of several emperors in succession, from Alexander to Decius inclusively, 152
—— who restored the tottering empire, 154
—— their lives begin to be more secure, 157-158
—— lead a life of greater indolence and less application to affairs, 158
—— wish to have themselves worshipped, 158
—— painted in different colors, depending on the passions of their historians, 161
—— many Greek emperors hated by their subjects on religious grounds, 197
—— dispositions of the peoples toward them, 198
—— revive theological disputes instead of quieting them, 209
—— let the navy go to ruin completely, 218
Empire, Roman: its establishment, 123 ff.
—— compared to the government of Algeria, 152
—— overrun by various barbarian peoples, 153
—— drives them back, and rids itself of them, 154
—— association of several princes in ruling the empire, 153, 157
—— partition of the empire, 159
—— of the East. See East.
—— of the West. See West.

T

Tarentines, an idle and pleasure-loving people, 29
—— descended from the Lacedaemonians, 44
Tarquin: how he ascends the throne; how he reigns, 25
—— his son violates Lucretia; effects of this outrage, 25
—— a more estimable prince than commonly believed, 26
Tartars (a people of) stops the Roman advance, 202
Taxes: Rome is freed of them, 150
—— they are reestablished at Rome, 150
—— never become more necessary than when a state is growing weaker, 171
—— carried, by the emperors, to an intolerable extreme, 171-172
Theodora (the empress) restores icon worship destroyed by the iconoclasts, 205
Theodosius the younger (the emperor): with what insolence Attila speaks of him, 177
Theologians, incapable of ever harmonizing their differences, 208
Thessalians, subjugated by the Macedonians, 57
Tiberius (the emperor) extends the sovereign power, 129
—— suspicious and distrustful, 129
—— under his empire the senate falls into a state of unspeakable baseness, 130
—— he takes the right of electing magistrates from the people in order to transfer it to himself, 131
—— whetther the degradation of the senate must be imputed to Tiberius, 131
Ticinus (battle of), unfortunate for the Romans, 50
Titus (the emperor) was the delight of the Roman people, 140
Trajan (the emperor), the most accomplished prince in the annals of history, 141
—— portrait of this prince; he makes war against the Parthians, 141
Trasimene (battle of), lost by the Romans, 50
Treasures amassed by princes, fatal to their successors: why, 149
—— treasures of the Ptolemies brought to Rome: effects they produced there, 160
Treaty, dishonorable, is never excusable, 62
Trebia (battle of), lost by the Romans, 50
Tribes: division of the people by tribes, 86
Tribunes: their creation, 84
—— emperors invested with the power of the tribunes, 131-132
Trinity (by reference to the) the Greeks get the idea they should have three emperors, 203
Triumph: its origin; how it influenced the growth of Roman greatness, 24
—— the basis of its being granted, 27
—— the use of the triumph abolished under Augustus: for what reason, 123
Triumvirate (first), 104